THE DAILY EXPRESS
GUIDE TO NAMES

Prospective parents often spend a lot of time discussing suitable names. You may agonise about having your baby at home or in hospital; you may lie awake at night wondering whether the family budget will run to a cot, a pram and a baby bouncer; you may dither about replacing your beloved MG Midget with a family estate car; but at least you can have some unalloyed fun in choosing your child's name.

It will not be the biggest decision in your life, but it will undoubtedly affect the way your child develops.

Every name has a character, a history and a tradition. With the help of this book you can select a name that will fit *your* child.

THE DAILY EXPRESS
GUIDE TO NAMES

Merle Jones

Star

A STAR BOOK

published by
the Paperback Division of
W. H. ALLEN & Co. Ltd

A Star Book
Published in 1981
by the Paperback Division of
W. H. Allen & Co. Ltd
A Howard and Wyndham Company
44 Hill Street, London W1X 8LB

Printed in Great Britain by
Hunt Barnard Printing Ltd., Aylesbury, Bucks.

ISBN 0 352 30813 3

TO MY MOTHER
For choosing well

INTRODUCTION

Would Alexander still have been the Great if he had been called Claude? Would Cleopatra have bewitched Antony as Queen Mildred? Helen's *face* might have launched a thousand ships if she had been known as Ethel of Troy but nobody would have written poetry about her. And how about Sidney the Conqueror, Basil the Hun, Romeo and Daisy or St Gladys of Arc?

The name bestowed on a child at birth moulds its personality. Many a fourteen-stone, five-foot-eleven, hockey-playing Gisele must have cursed the day she was baptised, and there have to be a few fat, spotty Tarquins who wish that less imaginative parents had called them Jim. It is tempting to go overboard when faced with the problem of naming a child; but before you get carried away and call your little bundle Hereward or Portia, just remember that *you* won't have to live with the name all your life. When they grow up, the kids will probably thank you for calling them John and Jane.

This book is designed to give parents a helping hand in choosing names discreetly. The glossary provides a wide choice of possibilities, and the introductory chapters attempt to show you which names wear well and which sound ridiculous as soon as the novelty of the new arrival has worn off.

Whether we care to admit it or not, there is considerable social snobbery involved in the choice of names; not simply class snobbery, but the snobbery of knowing what is fashionable, traditional or just plain awful. It is a snobbery of 'good taste' rather than what a less egalitarian age called good breeding. This book cannot claim to be the ultimate

7

authority in such matters, but at least it will give you some idea.

In the end, before you make your choice, remember one vital point. Never underestimate the effect of a name on its bearer. Your son or daughter will hear it hundreds of times every day. Children always find ways of making each other's lives a misery. Try not to give the others an edge over yours by providing them with names which will make them a laughing-stock. Something which sounds poetic at the christening can be hell in the playground.

CHAPTER ONE

THE BASIC GUIDELINES

You may agonise about having your baby at home or in hospital; you may lie awake at night wondering whether the family budget will run to a cot, a pram and a baby bouncer; you may dither about replacing your beloved MG Midget with a family estate car; but at least you can have some unalloyed fun in choosing your child's name.

Or can you?

It will not be the biggest decision in your life, but it will undoubtedly affect the way your child develops. Before choosing a name, some parents will work out the numerological significance of their tentative selections, in the hope of picking something which will have a beneficial effect on the child's life. There is an ancient practice, which still survives among some tribes, and in Middle Eastern communities, of giving a new-born child two names – the one which he will use all his life and a secret one, which is whispered in the baby's ear and never revealed to anyone else. It is believed that the 'real' name is a reflection of the bearer's soul, and that anyone who knew it would have power over him. I'm not suggesting that you should adopt such extreme methods, but those two examples might make you pause and reflect just how important a name is to any individual.

Prospective parents often spend a lot of time discussing suitable names. Unfortunately most of us devote more thought to the attractions of names in isolation rather than considering the way they sound combined with our surnames, the possibility of unfortunate nicknames and the disastrous results of some sequences of initials. (On this last point, consider the probable sufferings of Christine Olive Williams.)

9

Forename-surname combinations offer untold hazards to the unwary. The Mrs Sendalls who called her only son Clark should have been fined for lack of imagination. Far less obvious, but a much bigger problem, is the incongruity of certain Christian names when combined with surnames. Generally speaking, the more exotic the preferred forename, the more heavily the decision on whether to use it should rest on the nature of the surname. Remember that many of the really beautiful but somewhat fancy ancient names were used at a time when surnames either had not been invented, or were as grand as the forenames. It was all very well to be the beautiful Roxanne when that was *all* you had to be. When you have to be the beautiful Roxanne Thompson it's best to start considering how nice Elizabeth and Mary sound. Of course there are some very old names which are so simple that they sound perfect followed by the most prosaic modern surnames. Helen is one; Simon another. There are no hard and fast rules here. Just remember not to treat the Christian name in isolation.

One problem which appears virtually insoluble is that of nicknames. You cannot influence the nickname which derives from physical appearance; a red-haired child will be Ginger and a plump one Fatty whatever Christian names you choose. You are equally powerless to avoid the images associated with certain surnames: Mr and Mrs White's son will inevitably be Chalky, and the same goes for 'Dusty' Miller or 'Bunny' Warren.

The Welsh have a particular problem here, owing to the abundance of certain surnames, like Jones, Williams, Thomas, Evans and Davies. Often in the past each village had six or eight residents with the same surname, and a nickname system developed to distinguish them. Some characteristic – perhaps the husband's job, or a physical or spiritual quality – would be attached to each bearer of a particular name. Thus one found Jones the Milk, Thomas the Boot (a cobbler) and Evans the Meat. It is alleged that at the turn of the century Ystrad Mynach, a Glamorgan village, had one of the country's last town criers. He used to sprint from street to street, gathering an audience for the news, ringing a bell as he went. His nickname? Ianto Full Pelt. The custom is declining nowadays, partly due to the increasing incidence of English surnames in such communities, partly because greater informality has led to wider use of Christian names as well as surnames.

All nicknames of the physical type, or those associated with surnames, are inevitable. As a parent, you just have to hope they go away. They usually do once the child grows up. What you *can* do is to find a Christian name which is hard to adapt as a nickname. Nicknames derived from children's forenames invariably stay with them for life, with the result that a very attractive name is eclipsed for ever by an ugly contraction. If you choose carefully, you should be able to avoid this.

The more commonplace names invariably have built-in nicknames. Peter all too easily becomes Pete, and William, Bill. Some parents attempt to get around the difficulty by choosing a name which produces passable nicknames, but even that can lead to difficulties. One family I know called their son Antony, because they quite liked Tony, too. When he grew up, all his friends called him Ant.

The safest course is to try avoiding such diminutives altogether. One-syllable names are generally best for this. Clare, Keith, Bruce and Jane are good examples. Unfortunately, though, even this is not a universal rule. It's hard to prevent people from calling Charles Charlie. James becomes Jim and John, Jack with depressing ease.

About the best general guideline is that you should work out the possible corruptions of all your tentative name choices. If you detest particular contractions, strike the name which produces them from your list.

There are quite a number of names which have managed to avoid diminutives altogether. For girls these include Mary, Elsa, Lucy, Kay, Nina, Verity, Iris and Fay; for boys, Graham, Leo, Giles, Paul, Guy, Mark, Miles, and Simon. Parents who try to beat the system by using a nickname as the full form invariably find it bounces back on them. Jenny, Sandra, Sally and Kate usually get called Jen, Sandy, Sal and Katie by those who are never content to leave well alone.

If, in spite of all your efforts, the name you choose is replaced by a diminutive which you dislike, your only hope is to set your teeth and go on using the full form, whatever others do. If you are lucky, they'll eventually come round to your point of view.

A word of advice if you are thinking of more than one Christian name. It is quite reasonable if there is a family name which you want to preserve, or if you want to give your child the opportunity of changing later if he dislikes your first choice. Otherwise, in an age of application forms, John Smith finds life much easier than he would as John Albert George Smith.

Finally, don't allow yourself to be rushed into plumping for a name which you don't really like. When a child is born, some parents are so anxious to make a final decision that they snatch a name from thin air and father rushes off to register it before mother and child are out of hospital. Alternatively they have long conferences with family and friends and end up so confused that the final choice is an unwanted compromise or something totally unsuitable which appeals to strong-minded Aunt Grace.

Neither of these is an ideal method of selection. First, you will be wise to make it a husband-and-wife decision and not a committee affair. Second, make a firm choice before the birth, when you have plenty of time, and stick to it. Third, never assume the child's sex before it is born. Choose a name for a girl and one for a boy. Nothing dents a young girl's self-confidence more than to hear her father telling his friends that he called her Lesley ' . . . because I thought she'd be a boy, born with a rugger ball in his hands'. And don't think that a father would never be so cruel. They frequently are.

CHAPTER TWO

THE TRADITIONAL APPROACH

There is a lot to be said for tradition. Most parents are only too aware of the pitfalls of choosing a name which must suit their baby not only in childhood but throughout adult life. How can they possibly know whether the flower-faced infant asleep in her cot will grow up to be beautiful or plain, frail or fat? Certain names would be perfect if we could foresee the child as a fully-developed personality, but it is often safer to forsake the exotic in favour of the old and well-tried.

Don't imagine that this limits you to a bunch of dusty, over-used, unimaginative tags. There is a rich mine of lovely old names which, although given to thousands of new babies each year, retain their character.

Even if you take the most mundane examples, you have a collection of pleasant names. From 1660 to 1649 the three most common English girls' names were Elizabeth, Mary and Anne. More than three hundred years later, in 1976, Elizabeth was still at the top, according to *The Times*, which annually carries a popularity chart of the names used most frequently in its births column. Anne had slipped out of the top ten, but Mary was still there, in fourth place. The other most popular names in 1976 all had long traditions: they were Jane, Louise, Sarah, Lucy, Charlotte, Clare, Alexandra and Catherine.

For boys it was much the same story. Between 1600 and 1649 the most popular names were William, John and Thomas. In 1976 William was second, Thomas fifth and John sixth. James headed the list, and the others in the top ten were Edward, Alexander, Charles, Robert, David and Richard.

There are pitfalls, of course, even with traditional names. Jane, one of the most popular, is delightful for a girl who grows up to be pretty. One of the most glamorous women I know is the perfect Jane. But woe betide the less fortunate female of that name. She will inevitably end up as Plain Jane, and will hate it. The other disadvantage is that such names lend themselves to unattractive short forms more readily than any others. John almost automatically becomes Jack; Richard, Dick; Peter, Pete; David, Dave; Charles, perversely, Charlie; Michael, Mike; William, Bill or Billy; Thomas, Tom; Robert, Bob; Christopher, Chris; James, Jim.

Among the girls, Anne, Mary and Jane are usually exempt, but of the others, Elizabeth becomes Liz, Betty or one of endless contractions; Sarah, Sally; Caroline, Carrie; Charlotte, Lottie, and so on. Frances, a lovely old 16th-century name, ends up as Fran, or, worst of all, Fanny.

Determined parents have the remedy in their own hands. If they choose a popular traditional name because they like it, they must insist that the full form is always used. Their sons and daughters may go through their teens as Jim and Sue, but the chances are that by the time they reach their twenties, the children themselves will start insisting on the full forms, having realised that James and Susannah are the more attractive versions.

If you like the idea of tradition but find the most popular names too commonplace, a slight variation will often maintain the simple effect while making it less mundane. For example, Nicol was originally the chief English version of Nicholas. Today it is quite rare, but has the simplicity and traditional appeal of the popular form. You might consider that Mary is a little overworked. How about Miriam? That was the Hebrew original from which Mary developed. In most cases, less commonplace variations of popular names are included in the glossary entries.

In Britain, traditional names come from a variety of sources, because of the diversity of our origins. Greece, Rome, Israel, Germany, Scandinavia and Normandy have all made contributions. In addition a wide range of Scottish, Welsh and Irish classical names is available. A considerable advantage of this category is that your child can impose his own character on the name instead of being dominated by it, which is likely to happen if you choose something dramatic

14

that is indelibly associated with a specific personality.

The choice is so wide as to be confusing. One way of narrowing the field is to choose a handful of basic names, then work through all the variations until you find the right one. You can even borrow the equivalent from another language. For instance, if you call a boy Iain, you are simply naming him John in Gaelic. The French forms, Jean and Eugene, are probably best avoided, because when written it is hard to tell whether they belong to a boy or a girl; but there are still the Irish Sean or the Welsh Evan and Ieuan. Ivan is the Russian version, Hans the German. The frequently-used Jonathan is not, in fact, a derivation of John. It has different roots, but is an attractive name of a similar type.

Mary has numerous variations. The original Hebrew form, Miriam, was translated variously as Mariam, Marie, Maria, Marion and Mariot. The Irish version is Moire, the Welsh Mair. Molly, originally a pet form, became so popular that it is now an independent name. The Dutch Marijka is probably the prettiest version of all, but few British surnames suit it.

In general the traditional names are simple, basic and widely used. In any crowd the majority of people will have such names. Naturally the popularity of particular examples will vary with the times. Thomas, once among the most commonplace, has returned to favour so recently after a long eclipse, that it is positively trendy; and for once the short form, Tom, is quite attractive, too. William, out of favour since early this century, is currently very fashionable – but not when shortened to Bill or Billy.

Helen has been so universally popular for such a long time that it has developed a large number of variations, most of them attractive names in their own right. Among the best known are Ellen – once the usual English form – Eleanor, Elaine, Leonora, Helena and Elianor. Some of them may be a little too fancy for use with the more basic modern surnames, but otherwise they have no drawbacks.

If you like the traditional group but wish to avoid the really commonplace without resorting to fanciful derivations, there are many names which have been unfashionable for a long time and are now returning to favour. They include Edgar, Edmund, George, Henry and Timothy for boys; and

Alice, Amy, Christina, Diana, Harriet and Phyllis for girls.

So far we have talked about social tradition. There is also family tradition. It often gives parents a pleasant sense of continuity to choose an old family name, but they become discouraged when they consider the names of their own parents, aunts and uncles. If you have this problem, skip a generation and go back to your grandparents. Family Bibles, with their great lists of names on the flyleaves, are invaluable for this sort of research. Many of the names are unlikely to be suitable, but you could discover that generations of female ancestors used, say, Amy, or that a lot of the men were called Daniel.

This sort of name choice has two advantages: your child grows up with a traditional, non-fanciful name, and rich Great-Uncle George may leave Little George a packet in his will!

CHAPTER THREE

TODAY'S EMMA IS TOMORROW'S BERTHA

Walking through the toy department at Harrods on a Saturday afternoon, a foreigner might be forgiven for thinking that all English children were called Emma, Victoria, Gideon or Daniel. In fact these are just part of the latest crop of trendy names.

Trendy parents are a naming class on their own. They are to be found en masse in London and the Home Counties, and scattered pockets exist in the depths of the country, too. They are the people who have interesting homes in South West Something, or, in the countryside, poetic little labourers' cottages crammed with stripped pine furniture and knee-deep carpets. They are avid readers of the colour supplements.

Members of this group appear to have a highly-developed telepathic link on everything from kitchen crocks to literature, because periodically they all change their tastes simultaneously. The names they give their children are subject to similar conditions. The criterion for what is acceptable appears to have little to do with fashion. It is, rather, a feeling that a thing is just right for the current social mood. One sometimes suspects that their children's names are chosen not because they are appealing but because they sound right for the time. You may think that this is not the best way to select a name, but if you want to join the trendies, here are a few guidelines.

Along with Daniel and Gideon, Barnaby, Benedict and Alexander are already well established. Trendies who wish to give their sons a butch image from birth go in for the sturdy brevity of Jake, Ben and Luke. Dominic, once popular, is getting a bit tired now. It was worked to death in the late 1960s. Marcus and Matthew are both up and coming.

For girls, Emma is now almost as worn as Dominic. Samantha and Melanie are positively passé. They became too popular too quickly for the trendies, who have moved on to fresh pastures. Victoria is a safe choice – well, for the next year or two, anyway – and Abigail and Olivia are climbing the popularity chart.

If you want to start your own cult names, or be in on the early days of the latest examples, it's not difficult. As surely as the list of most-used names from the births columns of *The Times* gives a good idea of the favourite traditional choices, so the list of most-used *first* names gives you a rundown of the current crop of trendies. The two lists, published together in *The Times*'s correspondence column every January, are remarkably different, particularly the girls' names. The top ten for each sex for the previous year reported in January 1980 were as follows. The bracketed figures give the name's position the year before.

GIRLS	BOYS
Elizabeth (1)	James (1)
Louise (8)	Alexander (6)
Jane (3)	William (7)
Mary (5)	Thomas (3)
Sarah (2)	John (5)
Alice (–)	Edward (2)
Clare (7)	Charles (8)
Victoria (4)	David (9)
Katherine (–)	Robert (–)
Alexandra (–)	Richard (10)

Caroline, Helen and Anna, prominent in 1979, have fallen from favour, as has Nicholas.

Between 1973 and 1977 the battle for top position was between Emma and Sarah. But Emma, No. 1 in 1977, has now disappeared from the top ten completely. Sarah clearly has more staying power, although the more traditional Elizabeth is the current favourite and Louise is rising fast. But it's no use choosing either if you want to set a trend. You have to go for the new up-and-coming names. Alice is clearly the

Emma of the next few years, having soared into the list from nowhere. Alexandra is also a strong new contender.

On the male side, William and Robert have made the most remarkable progress, but they don't qualify as trendies because they have been traditional favourites for years outside smart circles. Bearing in mind that the boys' list always seems to change more slowly than the girls', you will probably be safely avant garde with any of the top five – on certain conditions. The names must *always* be James, Thomas, William, Alexander and John (you will just get away with Alex, but not Alec). Jimmy, Tommy, Bill and Jack are the exact opposites of what you are seeking. On general principle, the longer the name has been on the list, the less likely it is to have much more fashionable mileage in it. The secret is to sort out the latest arrivals which are different enough from the traditional favourites to be noticed.

Of course, *The Times*'s list is just a rough guide. There are other general points to bear in mind. Potential winners must have a reasonably long tradition; not for trendies the fashionable names of stage and screen. Second, if short forms are used, they should be diminutives of old names, and should be the children's proper names, not contractions used later. Again, Jake and Ben are good examples. There is nothing wrong with a fancy name, as long as it is not positively eccentric. Sebastian and Damian, for example, are unusual enough to be good choices, but without sounding outrageous.

Given your list of old established names, you must be selective. Cuthbert goes back to Anglo-Saxon days, but no trendy parent would use it. The average trendy would die rather than admit it, but the best guide is whether the name sounds right for the hero or heroine of a story in one of the better women's magazines. That really sorts out the Cyrils from the Jocelyns!

Don't rule out the 'ordinary' ancient names. Treated with respect they can be very smart. William is a perfect example of one that made it. Roland could be destined for similar eminence. Joseph has a reasonable ring. But if you choose from this category, remember the golden rule that the names are right only so long as they are used in full. Bill, Rowly and Joe are anything but appropriate to your image.

Look out for another rash of biblical names. Reuben, Jethro and Jesse could make a big come-back at any moment. Orlando, although non-biblical, is another safe choice.

Similar rules apply to trendy tags for girls, with an added caution. Never get too fancy. Oriana and Ottilia, for instance, are quite wrong. There are plenty of possibilities in English literature. Perdita and Cordelia, both used by Shakespeare, would fit the trendy scene perfectly. More recently, Candida was one of Bernard Shaw's heroines. It is a good choice. Then there are the old 'virtue' names which were favourites with the Puritans. As well as being acceptably smart, they are often very pretty. Verity, Patience and Charity are good examples. Royal names can be good trendies for girls – as long as you take them from before World War One. Alexandra, Sophie and Charlotte are perfect; Margaret Rose would be quite another matter.

Reversal of sex on an otherwise ordinary name can make it trendy. Robin is commonplace for a boy, but for a girl it makes the grade. Morgan is a splendid name for either sex, good and masculine for a boy (remember the pirate captain?) and faintly magical for a girl (Morgan-le-Fay was the great enchantress of Arthurian legend).

Really self-confident trendies can score over everyone by taking a pretty noun, not previously used as a proper name, and bestowing it on their child. Mick and Bianca Jagger managed it when they called their daughter Jade. Rain and India have been used successfully; so have Emerald and Opal (but *never* the Victorian favourites, Pearl and Ruby). The real danger here is that you might choose something that sounds too fancy, or just looks wrong. Unless you are absolutely sure of your ground, it's best to leave this category well alone. In any case, such names tend to be found among show business jetsetters, not throughout the colour supplement crowd.

One word of warning: trendies often name their children with a view to impressing friends or conforming with 'smart' taste. There are better reasons for choosing the label that will last a human being for life. Many fashionable names are very attractive in their own right. If you are looking for something chic, choose the name because you like it. A desire to impress the neighbours is a poor reason for calling your child Crispin; in a family of Shakespeare-lovers it would be understandable.

There is another very good reason for avoiding this type of name. When it goes out of fashion, it has been so over-used that it is stone dead for generations. The Victorians presented a perfect example of what happens when 'new' names are seized indiscriminately and done to death. The second half of the nineteenth century was very like the present period for name fashions. Ancient names were resurrected and suddenly became chic; words which had previously simply been nouns suddenly appeared as names; people committed acts of piracy on distinguished surnames and turned them into forenames. Traditionalists smote their brows in disgust and fulminated about the new crops of 'fancy' names which were displacing the old customary ones.

What were these names which created such a stir? There are too many to list fully here, but in general the smart names of Victorian and Edwardian days were the ones which make us wince today – Bertha, Gertrude, Mabel, Ada, Maud (after all, 'Come into the garden, Maud,' was a passionate ballad of romantic love, not a music hall send-up). Stanley, Herbert, Sydney and Humphrey are masculine examples. These names have been so devalued by over-use that it will probably be at least a couple of generations before they are revived, if ever. It is quite likely that a similar fate awaits Emma and Gideon.

CHAPTER FOUR

AND NOW FOR SOMETHING COMPLETELY DIFFERENT . . .

There will always be people for whom tradition and literature fail to provide names with enough drama and colour for their liking. They cast about for other sources, looking to films, television, pop music, sports personalities and foreign countries for inspiration. The results can be disastrous.

In the nineteenth century such people named their daughters Alma, after the battle in the Crimean War. The same sort of thing went on in the Boer War. I know of one poor soul who was christened Mafeking because she was born the night it was relieved. When she grew up she married a Mr Kronk. How would you like to go through life as Mafeking Kronk?

When Hollywood got going, it was responsible for the creation of more fancy names than any other institution in history. It was like an insatiable parent who could not be satisfied with ordinary names for its children. In went the would-be stars with everyday names; out came fully-fledged personalities, newly christened Rita, Judy, Jayne, Marilyn, Debra and Lana. The men were Clark, Kirk, Gregory, Errol, Cornel and Marlon. People loved it. They have been borrowing Hollywood's fantasy names for their own children ever since.

In the 1950s and 1960s, television added to this vast new repertoire. This time the fantasy was even wilder, because instead of borrowing the names of TV stars, people tended to go for the names of the fictional characters they portrayed. Thus we had a generation peppered with Cheyennes, Shanes and even Broncos.

Modern pop singers invent their names as freely as do

people in the film industry, so fans come up with equally fantastic choices.

Footballers generally have fairly prosaic names, so one would think that the sports fan's child, at least, would be safe from the craze. He is – except in the occasional case when Dad christens him after the whole Manchester United squad and the poor infant winds up with eleven names.

The enthusiasm for Continental names has also built up since the end of the last war, as people have begun to go abroad on holiday Juan, Giulietta and Emanuelle sound marvellous when spoken in a caressing foreign accent, and with an appropriately foreign surname following them. Enthusiasts forget all too readily that they sound a lot different pronounced in Cockney or Scouse and allied to a surname like Brown.

There's a moral for us all here. However tempting the exotic may seem, you almost invariably regret it in the end. Simplicity, tradition and the right language cannot be improved upon by the most imaginative invention.

You may wonder what is so terrible about naming your daughter Rita or Marilyn, or whatever the latest screen goddess is called. Nothing, except that she will have to live up to an impossible image all her life. It can be an awful burden. There is the added disadvantage for girls that a film star name is a terrible age giveaway in later years. If you are called Shirley, the chances are that you were born in the 1930s, when little Miss Temple was at the height of her fame. Rita is a 1940s girl; Marilyn saw the light of day in the 1950s. This holds good of people who are named after royalty and national heroes, too. No prizes for guessing the ages of Marina or Winston.

In the last analysis, it is you alone who choose the names of your children. Try to select the name for the child, and not to match the child to some romantic image in your head. Everyone will be happier in the end.

GLOSSARY

A

Aaron (m)
Of Hebrew or Egyptian origin, this was the name of Moses' brother, the first High Priest of Israel. It has always been unusual, although it was used in England after the Reformation. The meaning is unknown. Aaron goes well with modern surnames and could become popular if the current vogue for Biblical names continues. Beware of those who will try to shorten it to Ron.

Abel (m)
Derived from the Hebrew for 'son', this name was popular during the Middle Ages but is unusual today. Perhaps the fate of the first Abel – murder at the hand of his brother – makes parents think twice before using it. The surname Abell, Abelson and Nabbs developed from it. Nicknames are Abe and Abie.

Abigail (f)
Of biblical origins, Abigail was popular during the seventeenth century, but fell into disuse after becoming a slang term for a lady's maid. It is, however, a pretty name, and is rapidly becoming fashionable again. It combines readily with most surnames. Abbie and Gail are the diminutives, the latter having become more common as a modern name than the original full form. In Hebrew, Abigail means 'father rejoiced'.

Abner (m)
Don't use it unless you have fathered an American cartoon character. It also shortens all too readily to Ab or Abbie. Still occasionally used in the USA.

Abraham (m)
This has rather patriarchal associations. The popular contractions, Abie and Abe, are not really musical and the full
form sounds oddly dated when combined with modern surnames. The Hebrew meaning is 'father of a multitude'.

Absalom (m)
The unfortunate son of King David who led a rebellion
against his father and was killed while trapped by his long
hair in the branches of a tree. Although still used in France
(where it is spelled Absolon), the name is virtually extinct
in Britain. It comes from Hebrew words meaning 'father'
and 'peace'.

Acelin (m)
Very rare derivation of Old French Asce. Meaning unknown.
Choose it if you want a name for your child that no one else
shares.

Ada (f)
Had its day a century ago. Avoid it. It conjures up pictures
of mothballs and bombazine. The variation, Adah, is no
better.

Adam (m)
Formerly fashionable, now devalued. There are dozens of
Adams in every comprehensive school, but if you like the
name anyway, go ahead. It combines readily with most
surnames and does not lend itself to nicknames. In Hebrew,
Adam means 'red'.

Adela (f)
An ancient name, useful for those who want something
traditional but unusual. Derived from the Old German for
'noble', Adela was introduced to England by the Normans.
The French form, Adele, has been more widely used in
modern times, and as a result does not possess the cachet
of Adela.

Adelaide (f)
A delightful and, today, fairly unusual name, derived from

Adela. It was very popular in nineteenth-century England, thanks to William IV's 'good Queen Adelaide', but fell from favour as tastes changed. It is currently enjoying a well-deserved revival.

Adeline (f)
This has an old-fashioned ring, probably because it conjures up pictures of earnest Edwardian youths warbling *Sweet Adeline* around the piano after dinner. Nevertheless, that could be part of its charm. It is another derivative of the Old German for 'noble'. Like Adelaide, it became particularly popular in the nineteenth century. Variations include Adelina, Adelin and Edelina.

Adolphus (m)
The Welsh had a penchant for grand ancient names like this at the turn of the century, but what British surnames could possibly match it? Adolphus Jones has an unreal sound. The diminutive, Dolph, is deplorable. Even its meaning, 'noble wolf' in German, has unfortunate connotations.

Adrian (m), Adrienne (f)
A pleasant, traditional name, never popular enough in Britain to have become commonplace. Comes from the Latin 'of the Adriatic'. Adrienne, the best-known modern feminine form, is French. The traditional British variation, Adriana, is pretty and very unusual.

Aeneas (m)
According to legend, Aeneas was a Trojan hero who escaped the sack of Troy and later founded Rome. Its main use in Britain has been as a translation of the Gaelic Angus. It sounds wildly inappropriate with modern surnames. If you come from a family of classical scholars you will probably get away with it.

Agatha (f)
Extremely unfashionable at present, with a similar image to Ada's. It means 'good woman' in Greek and actually *sounds* as if it does! Somehow one cannot imagine an Agatha ever having any fun. The short form is Aggie.

Aglaia (f)
Another name more suitable in a family of classical scholars
than anywhere else. It is Greek for 'beauty' or 'splendour'
and is the name of one of the three Graces. Used only very
occasionally in England.

Agnes (f)
In Greek, 'pure' or 'chaste'. Once among the most popular
English names, it is uncommon today, probably because it
sounds dated. It has numerous variations which are more
appealing than the original. These include Annis, Annys,
Annais and Annot. Anis is still used as a gipsy name. The
Spanish form, Inez, is occasionally used in this country.
In Wales, the name developed as Nest or Nesta.

Aidan (m)
From Old Irish 'fire'. Attained some popularity in the nineteenth century and is enjoying a modern revival along with
many other Celtic names.

Aileen (f)
See Eileen.

Aimee (f)
See Amy.

Aine, Aithne (f)
See Eithne.

Alan (m), *Alanna* (f)
From the Irish meaning 'harmony'. The French forms,
Alain and Alein, first became popular in England after the
Norman Conquest. They developed as Alleyne, now a surname and, less often, a forename. Alan, Allan and Allen are
all widely used today. The Welsh form is Alun. Alanna, the
feminine form, is very uncommon. Think carefully before
you choose it. Your daughter – and everyone else – may
think you did so in disappointment that she was not a boy.
Al, the masculine diminutive, has a gangsterish ring.

Alaric (m)
Old German for 'Ruler of All'. An unusual name, popular with ancient Gothic kings. The best-known Alaric pillaged Rome in the fifth century. Hard to combine with English surnames, unless they are aristocratic.

Alastair (m)
See Alexander.

Alban (m)
Never popular, this, the name of the first British martyr, has a very aristocratic image. (I cannot guarantee that this will hold true for a child called Alban Biggs, however.) It simply means 'of Alba' in Latin.

Alberic (m)
See Aubrey.

Albert (m), *Alberta, Albertine* (f)
Never recovered from the Stanley Holloway monologue about a boy who had 'a stick with an 'orse's 'ead 'andle, the finest that Woolworths could sell . . . ' It is derived from an Old German name meaning 'noble and bright' and became popular in Britain when Queen Victoria married her Prince. Commonly abbreviated to Bert. The feminine forms have always been rare and Alberta is associated with the Canadian province rather than the Prince Consort.

Aldous (m)
From the Old German meaning 'old'. Very uncommon in Britain except in East Anglia, where it has been in use since the thirteenth century. Modern surnames like Aldiss and Aldhouse developed from it. A variation, Aldo, is still used quite frequently in North America.

Alec (m)
See Alexander.

Alethea, Althea (f)
Derived from the Greek for 'truth', Alethea became fashionable in England in the seventeenth century. Althea means

28

'wholesome' and is a different name. Uncommon today, it is an attractive name.

Alexander (m), *Alexandra* (f)
Names of distinction. Trendy *and* upper class. Never shorten the masculine form to Alec, although Alex is quite acceptable. It means 'defending men' and is of Greek origin. Sandra, originally a feminine diminutive, is now a name in its own right. It shares none of the virtues of the original. Alexander was early adopted into Gaelic as Alasdair, and is now often spelled phonetically as Alastair and Alisdair. Surnames like Saunders and Sanderson are derivations of Alexander.

Alexis (m), *Alexia* (f)
Greek 'helper', 'defender'. These developed mainly as Russian names. They have a rare quality among foreign names, in that they work very well with British surnames. Both names are attractive, dignified, classless and unusual.

Alfred (m)
Almost certain to be called Alf or Fred. If you can silence the nick-namers, Alfred itself is all right, but it will be an up-hill struggle. The name is of Old English origin, meaning 'elf counsel'. At present it is unfashionable. The Middle English variation, Avery, is very unusual.

Algernon (m)
Old Norman French name little used today. The awful diminutives, Algie and Algy, are good reasons for keeping it that way. It means 'with whiskers'. Incidentally, it's very aristocratic.

Alice (f)
An old name enjoying fashionable revival, Alice has some pretty variations. Adelise is the original form. Alicia and Alison are later developments. The name evolved from Adelaide. The attractive French form, Alix, is easily combined with English surnames.

29

Alicia (f)
See Alice.

Aline (f)
Developed from Adeline, Aline is unusual but more popular than the original form. Modern variations include Arleen and Arline.

Alison (f)
See Alice.

Alma (f)
Enjoyed a burst of popularity in the nineteenth century following the Battle of Alma. Also associated with the Latin adjective meaning 'loving'.

Aloysius (m)
Tony Hancock used it to raise laughs. Remember that.

Alphonso (m)
Old German, meaning 'noble ready'. Currently popular only in Spain and virtually unused in Britain.

Althea (f)
See Alethea.

Alwyn (m)
See Aylwin.

Amabel (f)
From the Latin Amabilis, 'lovable'. Passed into English language as amiable. Amabel is far prettier and less commonplace than the now dated short form, Mabel. It needs a fairly dignified surname to set it off properly. The diminutives Belle and Bella are rather vulgar.

Amanda (f)
Apparently coined by seventeenth century English dramatists from the Latin for 'lovable'. Widely used ever since. The pet form, Mandy, is bearable for a child, but can be a bore when she grows up.

Amaryllis (f)
English poets popularised this Greek literary name for a
country girl. It means 'fresh stream'. Pretty, very uncommon,
but almost impossible to combine successfully with a surname.

Ambrose (m), *Ambrosine* (f)
Always unusual, this derivation from the Greek for 'divine'
is now virtually extinct. The Welsh form, Emrys, is far more
popular, but not in England.

Amelia (f)
Pretty derivation from Old German, of uncertain meaning.
One of the English forms, Emily, is currently enjoying a
fashionable revival and Amelia could become equally
popular. The modern German and French forms, respectively Amalie and Amelie, are also very attractive. It became
popular in England under the Hanoverians.

Amos (m)
This was one of the Old Testament names adopted by the
Puritans in England when saints' names became unpopular
after the Reformation. Its popularity in Britain declined but
it is still used in the USA. Amos is derived from the Hebrew
'carried'.

Amy (f)
Derived from the French, meaning 'beloved woman', this is
a perfect name for a beautiful daughter. It is pleasant, not
over-used, and goes well with practically all surnames. The
French form, Aimee, though pretty, is rather fancy.

Amyas (m)
Its origins are uncertain, but possibly this is a masculine
form of Amy. It has never been very widely used, but
enjoyed a revival thanks to Kingsley's novel *Westward Ho!*,
with its hero, Amyas Leigh, in the 1850s.

Anastasia (f)
Probably best known as the name of the youngest daughter
of the Tzar Nicholas II, whom some people believe to have

escaped the massacre of her family following the Russian Revolution. The name has Greek origins and means 'resurrection'. Historically more popular in Ireland than in England. It has been used to translate the Irish Aine.

Anchoret (f)
See Angharad.

Andrea (f)
Fairly modern feminine equivalent of Andrew. Although it is found in old records, it is likely that the spoken form was originally Andrew for girls as well as boys. Andrea is uncommon, although the French form, Andrée, has been fairly widely used here.

Andrew (m)
A much-loved traditional name, derived from the Greek for 'manly', and borne by the patron saints of Scotland and Russia. Andy, Drew and (in Scotland) Dandy are popular diminutives. If you like the name but find it too commonplace, you might prefer the Russian form, Andrei.

Aneurin (m)
Popular Welsh name, possibly derived from the Latin Honorius, meaning 'honourable'. Nye is the diminutive. The alternative spelling, Aneirin, though now less common, is traditionally the correct form.

Angel (m)
Traditionally a West Country name in Britain, but little used elsewhere. The best-known occurrence of the name is Angel Clare in *Tess of the D'Urbevilles*. Occasionally used instead of Angela as a woman's name.

Angela (f)
Female form of Angel. Very popular in Britain since the nineteenth century, but little used before then. An attractive name, it can be ruined by the ghastly diminutives Ange and Angie.

Angelica (f)
From Latin meaning 'angelic', it has never been as popular here as its equivalent, Angelique, in France.

Angharad (f)
An ancient Welsh name which could be regarded as the Celtic equivalent of Amanda, as it means 'much-loved'. Angharad was adapted by the English to make Anchoret, Ancret, Ankerita and Ingaret.

Angus (m)
See Aeneas.

Ann, Anna, Anne (f)
Traditionally the name given to the mother of the Blessed Virgin. This is the Western form of the Hebrew Hannah, the original always having been unusual in Britain outside Ireland. Ann is a pleasant name but has been used so often that it is now somewhat undistinguished. Anna and Annette are less commonplace, and the French and Spanish Nanette and Anita reasonably unusual. Annot was a common form in Medieval Britain. Early popular pet forms, Nan and Nanny, were replaced by Nancy when they became synonyms for loose women. At various times Anne has been used as part of a double name with Mary, either as Mary-Anne or Anne-Marie. Its Hebrew meaning is 'God has favoured me'; 'Grace' is a subsequent interpretation.

Annabel, Annabella (f)
Annabel is an ancient Scottish name, latinized as Annabella, which, curiously, was unknown on the Continent until modern times. It appears to be unconnected with Anne, but to be a development of Amabel. A pretty and popular name, but again, watch out for the diminutives Belle and Bella.

Anne, Annette (f)
See Ann.

Annis (f)
See Agnes.

3   33

Anthea (f)
From the Greek adjective 'flowery'. First used as a Christian
name in Britain in the seventeenth century, when it was
popular with poets. Never common. Be prepared for people
to shorten it to Thea.

Antoinette, Antonia (f)
These slightly regal-sounding names are, respectively, the
French and Italian diminutive feminine forms of Antony.
Both became popular in England during the nineteenth
century. Antonia is rather more aristocratic than Antoinette,
as Toinette, the main nickname derived from the latter, has
a film starlet ring. Both require the right surname to set
them off properly.

Antony, Anthony (m)
The name of a Roman clan, this has unknown origins.
Antony is the original spelling, Anthony appearing only after
the Renaissance, when it was assumed that the name derived
from 'Anthos', Greek for 'flower'. In pronunciation the 'h'
should always be silent, so it is probably wisest to use the
original form. Although always popular, the name has not
been over-used. Its main disadvantage is the almost universal use of its unattractive short form, Tony. A modern
feminine diminutive, Toni, is even more objectionable.

Aphra (f)
Now almost extinct, this name became popular in the seventeenth century, thanks to popular misunderstanding of a
passage in the Book of Micah: 'In the house of Aphrah roll
thyself in the dust . . . ' In fact, Aphrah means dust in
Hebrew.

April (f)
A modern name, from the name of the month. Although it is
the prettiest of this type of derivation (May and June are
more commonplace and more dated), avoid it if you want a
name with a long tradition. The French form, Avril, is more
widely used.

Arabel, Arabella (f)
There is a faint possibility that this derives from an ancient name for Arabia, but this is unlikely. Like Annabel, Arabella is most frequently encountered in Scotland. Arbell was an early variation.

Archibald (m)
Used in England since before the Norman Conquest, Archibald means 'true and bold' in Old German. Over the centuries it has been used primarily in Scotland. Archie is the usual diminutive.

Ariadne (f)
A splendidly aristocratic name of unknown origin. The Ariadne of Greek mythology was the daughter of the king of Crete who helped Theseus to escape from the labyrinth by giving him thread to lay a trail. The Italian and French forms, Arianna and Ariane, are less regal and very pretty. All are unusual in Britain.

Arleen, Arline (f)
See Aline.

Arminel (f)
Very rare name of unknown origin, still used in Devon.

Arnold (m)
Old German combination of 'eagle' and 'power'. It fell out of fashion in Britain after the Middle Ages, but survived as a surname and enjoyed a return to popularity in the nineteenth century. It is fairly common today. In the USA Arnie is used as a diminutive.

Artemesia (f)
Greek for 'belonging to Artemis'. Artemis was the Greek Diana, goddess of the hunt and wild animals. Artemesia was first used in Britain in the eighteenth century. Today it survives almost entirely as a traditional name with certain families.

Arthur (m)
The legendary king who is Britain's greatest romantic figure bore this name. Its origins are obscure. Arthur has been claimed as Celtic but is probably Roman. It became extremely popular during the nineteenth century, partly out of the popularity of Arthur Wellesley, Duke of Wellington, partly due to renewed interest in the Arthurian legend. The short forms are Art and Artie, both heard more frequently in the USA than in Britain.

Aspasia (f)
Always very uncommon, this name was coined by seventeenth century dramatists. In Greek it means 'welcome'. Although it sounds grand, it was used at least once by humble folk. In her *History of Christian Names* (1863), Charlotte Mary Yonge recalls meeting a village child whose mother said, 'Her name's Aspasia, but us calls her Spash.'

Astrid (f)
Scandinavian name of ancient origin which has become fairly popular in this country since the turn of the century. In Old German it means 'God-strength'.

Athene (f)
Name of the Greek goddess of war and peace, later the Roman goddess of wisdom. Occasionally used as a girl's name in Britain, it requires a very distinguished surname.

Auberon (m)
See Aubrey.

Aubrey (m)
Derived from the Old German Alberic – 'elf-ruler' – this name was introduced to Britain by the Normans. Albery was a variation and the medieval diminutive, Auberon, was adapted by Shakespeare for his king of the fairies in *A Midsummer Night's Dream*. It fell out of general use but was revived in the nineteenth century. Aubrey is still fairly unusual.

36

Audrey (f)
Started life as a pet name for Etheldreda, then replaced it. (If you were called Etheldreda, wouldn't you prefer Audrey?) The word 'tawdry' derives from it indirectly, as a term coined to describe the shoddy goods sold at St Etheldreda's fair. It enjoyed a revival earlier this century and is very commonplace today. In Old English it means 'noble strength'.

Augustine, Austin (m)
Popular during the Middle Ages. Austin is the contracted form, and is probably more attractive to modern ears than Augustine. It means 'venerable' in Latin. Austin is more commonly found as a surname than as a Christian name today, but still occurs.

Augustus (m), *Augusta* (f)
Similar derivation to Augustine. This name was adopted by German princes and introduced to Britain by the Hanoverians. The feminine form was popular early in the nineteenth century. It is commonly shortened to Gus or Gussie.

Aurelia (f)
Pretty name derived from the Latin for 'gold'. The French version, Aurelie, is even more attractive. If you have a golden girl, here's the ideal name for her. A masculine version, Aurelian, has been used in Britain, but only rarely.

Averil (m and f)
Not to be confused with Avril, Averil has a different origin. It means 'battle' in Old English and was used as a girl's name until the seventeenth century. Since then it has been rare, but was used in the USA as a masculine name (eg Averell Harriman).

Avery (m)
See Alfred.

Avice, Avis (f)
Old Norman name of obscure meaning. It has been unusual

since the eighteenth century, but is still used occasionally, invariably spelled Avis.

Avril (f)
See April.

Aylmer (m)
An ancient name, common before the Norman Conquest. Today it is found as a surname more often than as a forename. It is derived from Aethelmaer, meaning 'noble and famous'. The popular American Christian name Elmer developed from it.

Aylwin, Aylwyn (m)
An Old English name meaning 'noble friend'. It is the root of various surnames. Alvin is a variation.

B

Babette (f)
See Elizabeth.

Babs (f)
See Barbara.

Baldric (m)
Introduced to England at the time of the Norman Conquest. Very rare today. Derived from Old German, it means 'old ruler'.

Baldwin (m)
Far more common nowadays as a surname than as a Christian name. Baldwin is Old German for 'brave friend'. As well as the original form, surnames like Bowden and Bodkin are derived from it. The name has always been popular in

Belgium in the continental form Baudouin, which is borne by the country's present king.

Balthasar (m)
A magnificent ancient name from the Old Testament. Belshazzar was the original form. Balthasar, Caspar and Melchior were the names ascribed to the three magi who followed the star to Bethlehem. Balthasar has been used only rarely in England.

Barbara (f)
Of Greek origin, meaning 'strange' or 'foreign', Barbara is popular again this century after being out of fashion for about three hundred years. It is the name of one of the four great virgin saints, but the most infamous Barbara in English history, the Duchess of Cleveland, was anything but virginal. She was Charles II's most celebrated mistress, and almost universally hated in London for her corrupt influence at court. She bore the king five children before he pensioned her off when her behaviour became too outrageous to be ignored. The traditional English form of the name is Barbary, pretty enough to deserve revival. Bab and Babs are the common British diminutives. In America and Australia, Barbie and Barb also occur. None is a desirable alternative to the full form. The fashionable modern spelling, Barbra, has no historical basis.

Bardolph (m)
Now rare as a forename, this is more usual as a surname. It derives from the Old German 'bright wolf'.

Barnabas, Barnaby (m)
Barnaby is currently in high favour with trendies. Barnabas, though still found, is for some reason less popular. It is only fashionable when used in full. Barney conjures up memories of old radio programmes ('Give 'im the money, Barney . . . '). Barnabas comes from Hebrew, and means 'son of consolation'. It is the name of St Paul's companion on his missionary journeys. Barnaby is the traditional English form. It combines well with most British surnames, particularly with the simple ones.

Barnard, Barnet (m)
See Bernard.

Barret, Barrett (m)
An old German forename which developed later to be used predominantly as a surname. It means 'bear ruler'.

Barry (m)
Of Irish origin, this name is so popular in Australia that it is now indelibly associated with that country. It means 'spear'. Although in general use, it is not fashionable. Does not lend itself to development of short forms.

Bartholomew (m)
There are 165 churches in England dedicated to St Bartholomew, and the name was very popular here after the Norman Conquest. In Hebrew it means 'son of Talmai'. Bartle, Bart and Bat are recognised short forms, and it is only in the latter two of these that the name survives in the USA today. In Britain it is obsolete, but is found extensively as a surname, with numerous derivations like Bartlett, Bates, Bateson and Batty.

Basil (m)
From the Greek meaning 'kingly'. For some reason this name developed an image similar to that suffered by names like Cedric, Cyril and Eustace, conjuring up a picture of anaemic young men in Victorian conservatories. In fact it is an ancient, regal name, as its meaning suggests. The feminine forms Basilia and Basilie were common in the Middle Ages but are obsolete today.

Bathsheba (f)
'Voluptuous' in Hebrew, this was the name of Uriah's wife, who afterwards married King David. Has occurred in Britain as a girl's name both in its original form, and as Barsabe and Bathshua. It is very uncommon today, and if you try matching it with any British surname you will understand why.

Beata (f)
A pleasant name, always uncommon in Britain. It means

'happy' in Latin. The name has been used occasionally since the twelfth century. Quite attractive when it accompanies a grand surname.

Beatrice, Beatrix (f)
The second spelling is the correct one, derived from Latin, 'bringer of joy'. Beautrice and Betteresse are English variations. Bettrys, the Welsh form, is still found occasionally. Beatty, Bee and Trixie are the usual short forms, but, thankfully, it is generally used in full nowadays.

Bedelia (f)
For some obscure reason, this name is sometimes used in Ireland as a genteel version of Bridget. It is very seldom found elsewhere, apart from the USA, where it is used as a name in its own right.

Belinda (f)
Like Linda, this attractive old name is derived from the Old German for 'snake'. The name first occurs in the old stories of Charlemagne, in which Belinda was the wife of the paladin Roland. It did not come into general use for centuries, achieving popularity when Pope used it for the heroine of his *Rape of the Lock*. It is a charming name which has never become commonplace. Bel is the usual diminutive, but Linda and Lindy are also used.

Benedict, Bennet (m), Benedicta (f)
After years of neglect, Benedict soared back into favour with the trendy names of the 1960s, but managed to avoid the over-use to which its co-favourite, Dominic, was subjected. It is an attractive name, derived from the Latin for 'blessed'. Traditionally the English form was Bennet, which is found as a surname today, but seldom as a Christian name. It is worth reviving, possibly for a daughter, as it was used for girls for a couple of centuries. Benedicta, the original feminine form, is now obsolete, but the Spanish version, Benita, has been introduced from the USA to Britain and combines reasonably with British surnames.

41

Benjamin (m)
Benjamin in the Bible was the youngest, much-loved son of Jacob, Benoni, the original Hebrew form, means 'son of my sorrow'. It was later changed to Benjamin, 'son of the right hand'. Like most biblical names, Benjamin declined early this century and is now enjoying a fashionable revival. The diminutive Ben now often appears as a name in its own right, and is equally favoured. Benny and Benjy are also traditional pet forms.

Bennet (m)
See Benedict.

Berenger (m)
One of Charlemagne's paladins in the old romances. The name is practically obsolete, but survives in places as a traditional family forename.

Berenice (f)
An attractive name often spoiled by pronunciation as a two-syllable word instead of the correct three syllables. It is derived from the Greek 'bringer of victory'. Bernice is a modern variation which does not share the distinction of the original, and lends itself to the awful diminutive, Bern.

Bernadette (f)
A French feminine derivation of Bernard. It is popular in Britain mainly among Roman Catholics, who use it in commemoration of St Bernadette Soubirous of Lourdes.

Bernard (m)
An Old German name whose meaning implied strength and courage, Bernard was very popular in the Middle Ages. It is still used quite widely, but has little distinction and is all too readily shortened to Bernie.

Bertha (f)
An old Frankish name meaning 'bright', which went out with the Middle Ages and was not revived until the nineteenth century. It shares Ada's mothball image, and was not aided by the fact that an enormous World War One field gun was christened Big Bertha.

Bertram (m)
In use here since the Middle Ages, this name has a somewhat pompous sound. It means 'bright raven' in Old
German. Bertram is uncommon today and likely to remain
so. The old diminutive, Berry, is more attractive, and
might have possibilities as a name in its own right. Bert and
Bertie are the more usual short forms. Bertrand, originally
the French form, is now a separate British name.

Bertrand (m)
See Bertram.

Beryl (f)
A modern name adapted from the precious stone which in
turn took its name from the Arabic for 'crystal'. Beryl offers
a salutary lesson in the inadvisability of choosing fanciful
names. It came into fashion in the first few decades of the
twentieth century, with no previous tradition, and has now
virtually ceased to be used. As a result it has an unattractive,
dated quality.

Bessie, Beth, Betsy, Betty (f)
See Elizabeth.

Bethia (f)
A Biblical name more popular in Scotland than elsewhere.
From the Hebrew meaning 'daughter of Jehovah'. It has
been used as a Christian name since the seventeenth century.

Bettina (f)
A modern name derived from Betty, a diminutive of Elizabeth, with a suffix.

Bevis (m)
For some reason this name sounds as if it belongs squarely
with inventions of the twentieth century, but in fact it has a
very ancient tradition. It is of Frankish origin and was introduced to Britain by the Normans. Bevis is still used today
but is rare. Its meaning is obscure.

43

Bianca (f)
See Blanche.

Blanche (f)
The feminine form of the French adjective meaning 'white'.
It appears as a translation of the Latin name Candida. It has
never been common in Britain, although it has been used
occasionally since the thirteenth century. The poet Chaucer
immortalised Blanche, Duchess of Lancaster, in his verse.
By the early nineteenth century it was regarded as a
romantic, old-fashioned name, and enjoyed something of a
revival. The Italian form, Bianca, is occasionally found in
England.

Blodwen (f)
Once very popular in Wales, Blodwen means 'white flower'.
Today it is fairly uncommon even within the principality
and almost never found elsewhere in Britain. Possibly the
ghastly diminutive, Blod, is to blame for this.

Bonamy (m)
A French surname derived from combination of the words
for 'good friend', Bonamy was used as a Christian name by
the Dobrées of Guernsey, after an heiress of that name
married into the family. Since then it has been used regularly
by the family and by people connected with it by marriage.

Bonny (f)
Modern Christian name, presumably derived from the use
of 'bonny' as an adjective. In Wales it has been used as a
diminutive for Bronwen.

Boris (m)
A popular Russian name meaning 'fight', sometimes used in
Britain this century.

Bram (m)
A mainly American diminutive of Abraham.

Branwen (f)
Branwen means 'white raven' in Welsh. The name is an

ancient one still used regularly in Wales. It has also evolved into a surname as Brangwyn.

Brenda (f)
This originated in Shetland. Brenda is derived from the Old Norse for 'sword'. It has been used widely since the nineteenth century, when Sir Walter Scott introduced a heroine called Brenda in his novel *The Pirate*. Today it is still in general use but is not fashionable.

Brendan (m)
If you like ethnic-sounding names, this is a good one, with old Irish origins. But be reticent about divulging its meaning – 'stinking hair'. No parents would be too popular with their son if his classmates discovered that! Incidentally, the Irish St Brendan has been credited with the discovery of America.

Brian, Bryan (m)
A Celtic name always particularly popular in Ireland due to the national hero, Brian Boru. It also became popular in medieval England, but disappeared in Tudor times, to be re-introduced from Ireland in the eighteenth century. Brian is still widely used. Its meaning is obscure.

Bridget, Brigid (f)
Brighid was the Celtic fire goddess, and means 'the high one'. Devotees appear to have regarded her with similar reverence to that given by Christians to the Virgin Mary, hence the name was considered too sacred for ordinary use for long periods. Bridget is the English version, Brigit and later Brigid the Old Irish. The modern Irish form is Brighid. With Mary, it is the most common name in modern Ireland. Biddy is the pet form. The Swedish Birgitte is a separate derivation, not a translation.

Bronwen (f)
Old Welsh name, meaning 'white breast'. It is still widely used in Wales, often abbreviated to Bonny.

Bruce (m)
A Scottish surname which spread to England in the Middle
Ages but was not adopted as a Christian name in either
country until the nineteenth century. It is a popular name
today, particularly in Scotland. It is derived from a place-
name, Braose, near Falaise in northern France.

Brunhild (f)
Introduced to England during the nineteenth century when
Wagner's operas became popular. Not much used today,
probably due to association of the name with bulky
Valkyries in horned helmets and the fact that it means 'battle
corset' in Old German.

Bruno (m)
Still used in Britain, but very rarely, Bruno is derived from
the Old German for 'brown'. The English surname Brown
is derived from the French nickname le brun, not from
Bruno.

Bryony (f)
A modern name, one of the more unusual examples adapted
from plant and flower names.

C

Cadwallader (m)
A traditional Welsh name meaning 'battle chief'. It has a
distinguished ring, but is somewhat unwieldly for modern
use. In any case, it cries out to be shortened to Cad. Still
found in Wales, it also occurs in North America.

Caleb (m)
Quite popular from the Reformation until the nineteenth
century, this name appears to have gone out of use in
Britain outside Scotland. However, it is simple, dignified and

has a long tradition – it is derived from the Hebrew meaning 'bold' or 'impetuous'. With biblical names enjoying fresh popularity it could be due for a come-back. Even the diminutive, Cal, sounds less objectionable than the short forms suffered by some other names.

Calvin (m)
Protestants took up Calvin as a surname in honour of John Calvin, the great religious reformer. It has enjoyed fairly wide use in North America but in Britain it appears to be confined to Scotland.

Cameron (m)
A Scottish clan name from the Gaelic 'crooked nose', Cameron is now found occasionally as a Christian name, again, chiefly in Scotland.

Camilla (f)
Always uncommon, this ancient name has roots in the Etruscan civilisation. It became fairly popular thanks to the Greta Garbo film *Camille*, but is very rare today.

Candace (f)
Surprisingly, this name was not invented last week for an emerging movie star. It appears to have been an ancient dynastic title for the queens of Ethiopia, and has been used as a Christian name in this country since the seventeenth century. It is pronounced Candiss. Before you decide on this very pretty name, remember that it will inevitably be shortened to Candy, which will be fine if your daughter grows up a delicious little sexpot and terrible if she has a weight problem.

Candida (f)
The Latin form of 'white' (See Blanche). An extremely attractive, distinguished name, apparently unused in Britain until Bernard Shaw used it for the heroine of a play. It is still unusual. Another name that should be treated with care if you are to avoid having a daughter called Candy.

47

Cara (f)
A direct adoption of the Italian word for 'dear', occasionally used as a British forename in the twentieth century. In Irish it means 'friend', and the Welsh word for 'darling', 'cariad', is similar. The Latin form, Carita, is charming.

Caradoc (m)
From the Welsh meaning 'amiable', this name is still found in Wales. In England it appears as the surname Craddock.

Carl (m)
See Charles.

Carla (f)
See Caroline.

Carlotta (f)
See Charlotte.

Carmel (f)
Hebrew for 'garden', and the name of a mountain in Israel. The use of Carmel as a forename is largely confined to Roman Catholics. Carmela and Carmelita are the variations.

Carmen, Charmaine (f)
Respectively of Spanish and French origin, their derivation is obscure, but both forms probably developed from the Latin word for 'song'. Carmen is a Spanish borrowing, used here occasionally since the Bizet opera of that name became popular in the nineteenth century. Charmaine is inseparable from memories of a somewhat sugary pop song of the 1950s vintage.

Carol (f)
A fairly recent addition to British forenames, it was introduced from the USA. It is probably a shortened form of Caroline, which has a much older tradition.

Carola (f)
See Caroline.

Caroline (f)
George II's queen, Caroline of Brandenburg-Anspach, introduced this name to Britain. It originated as the Italian feminine form of Charles, Carolina. Carola had achieved some popularity in the seventeenth century as a feminine form of Charles, used in Cavalier families, but Caroline has been much more widely used. Carolyn is a modern variation, as is Carla. Carrie, Caro, Lina and Lyn are the usual diminutives.

Casper (m)
See Jasper.

Cassandra (f)
The first Cassandra was the daughter of Priam, king of Troy. According to the legend, she was given the gift of prophesy, but it was made worthless by the condition that no one would ever believe what she said. The name became popular in Britain during the Middle Ages, when the Trojan War was a favourite subject of the poets. It never quite died out and is still used occasionally. If you choose it, try to see that the full form is always used. Cass, Sandy and Sandra lack its distinction.

Catharine, Catherine (f)
See Katherine.

Catriona (f)
See Katherine.

Cecil (m), *Cecilia, Cecily, Cicely, Celia* (f)
The masculine form was quite popular in medieval Britain, but never as fashionable as the feminine variations. Both developed from the Latin word for 'blind'. The masculine form enjoyed a revival at the end of the nineteenth century. Certain of the feminine forms have never lost their appeal. Cecilia was the patron saint of music. The name was introduced here after the Norman Conquest. Cicely and Sisley were the original English forms. Sela and Sely were pretty early short forms, never heard today. Ciss and Cissie are the common modern diminutives.

4   49

Cedric (m)
Allegedly invented by Sir Walter Scott in a novel when he mistook the Saxon name Cerdic for it. The infamous Victorian hero, Little Lord Fauntleroy, was called Cedric, which could explain why the name is not very fashionable today.

Celeste (f)
Another girl's name with a Hollywood aura, possibly by subconscious association with its Latin root – 'heavenly'. It is quite popular in France, where the derivation Celestine is also used.

Celia (f)
See Cecilia.

Ceridwen, Ceri (f)
Ceridwen was the Welsh goddess of poetry. The name has also been interpreted as a translation – 'white poetess'. It has always been quite popular in Wales, recently more in the diminutive form Ceri than in the full version.

Charis (f)
Became popular in the seventeenth century. Charis means 'grace' in Greek. It was never popular and is used only very occasionally today.

Charity (f)
Another of the Puritan virtue names. Caritas, from which the name derives, is Latin for 'Christian love'. When it was most popular, in the seventeenth century, parents sometimes went the whole hog and named triplets Faith, Hope and Charity. Perhaps that was overdoing things somewhat. Nevertheless, Charity is a pretty name, uncommon today, which could well be due for revival. Cherry is sometimes used as a pet form.

Charles (m)
In Old German and Old English this name meant, literally, 'a man'. It achieved universal popularity in Europe as the name of Charlemagne, founder of the Holy Roman Empire, and

has a different form for practically every Continental country. The French, like the modern English version, is Charles; the Italian Carlo; Spanish Carlos; German and Scandinavian, Karl; Dutch and Slav, Karel. It was not a popular name in England before the Stuarts, although it had been introduced by the Normans. In the nineteenth century it became really popular, sadly often in the pet form Charlie. Charles is a very fashionable name today, usually in its full form. Charlie and the alternative pet form Chas are still found, but best avoided. The Welsh short form, Charl, is an abomination. The name has been in *The Times* top ten for some years. Carl, a modern variation of the German form, is now popular.

Charlotte (f)
A feminine form of Charles with a long, distinguished tradition. Charlotte became popular in Britain after George III married Charlotte Sophia of Mecklenburg-Strelitz. George IV's daughter also bore the name. It was probably originally pronounced Charlotta. Its popularity declined somewhat early this century, but it has enjoyed a fashionable revival. Lottie is the usual pet form, although both Charlie and Carly have been used lately.

Charmaine (f)
See Carmen.

Charmian (f)
This should be pronounced Karmian, not Sharmian, as seems to be usual these days. The name is of Greek origin, meaning 'a little joy'. In Greece it was a neuter name, given to slaves. It has enjoyed a certain popularity in modern times, but is not fashionable.

Chauncey (m)
A surname of French origin, which moved to England and thence to the USA. There it has been used as a first name since the seventeenth century, and has occurred occasionally in Anglo-American families living in Britain.

51

Cherry (f)
See Charity.

Chloë (f)
The Greek goddess Demeter sometimes bore this name, which means 'a young green shoot'. It is mentioned in one of St Paul's Epistles, and from this source it was introduced to England in the seventeenth century. Although still used here, it is far more popular in American black communities.

Christabel (f)
A beautiful name which was lent added glamour and mystery when Coleridge used it in his most romantic poem. It is derived from the Latin Christabella – 'beautiful Christian'. Although it has been used in Britain since the sixteenth century, its occasional popularity today arises from its use by Coleridge. Mrs Pankhurst's elder daughter, a militant women's rights campaigner, was called Christabel. Chrissy and, more attractively, Christy, are the usual diminutives, but Christabel is too lovely a name to be wasted with abbreviations.

Christen (f)
See Christian.

Christian (m and f), *Christiana* (f)
A direct adaptation of the noun/adjective. This did not exist in English before the sixteenth century, appearing instead as Christen. This was occasionally used as a name, too. Occurrence of Christiana as a name before the sixteenth century points to a derivation from Latin. In Scotland, Kirsty is used as a pet form. The masculine form was never commonplace. Christiana gradually became more popular than Christian as a girl's name and both have been superseded today by Christina. All forms are commonly shortened to Chris and Chrissy. Tina is an abbreviation of Christina, although it often appears as a separate name nowadays.

Christine, Christina (f)
See Christian.

Christmas (m and f)
Sometimes used for children born on Christmas Day, more
usually for boys than for girls. Since the Middle Ages the
names of the great religious festivals have been used for
children born on the appropriate days. Christmas was the
most popular, but Pentecost and Easter were used, too. In
modern times Christmas has been virtually replaced by the
French equivalent, Noel.

Christopher (m)
All early Christians applied the Greek version of Christopher
to themselves. It means 'bearing Christ', and they took it as
meaning that they carried Christ in their hearts. Its first
recorded use as a forename is for an early Christian martyr.
His name was attached to the tale of a giant holy man who
bore the child Christ across a river, and St Christopher
became the patron of travellers. The name has been popular
for centuries. It appears as Christophe in French, Christoph
in German, Cristoforo in Italian and Cristobal in Spanish.
The sight of an image of St Christopher was thought to
protect the viewer from accident and death for the rest of
the day, so his picture frequently appeared on the outside of
houses in Catholic countries. In England he was a popular
subject with mural painters for the same reason. There are
attractive variations on the basic name. Kit and Kester are
found as early as the eighteenth century. In Scotland,
Chrystal appears as a variation. Chris is the most common
modern short form.

Chrystal, Crystal (m)
See Christopher.

Cicely (f)
See Cecilia.

Cindy (f)
See Lucinda.

Clara, Clare, Claire (f)
Clara has a decidedly dated ring to modern ears – possibly
because it was so popular in late Victorian and Edwardian

days that the 1920s seemed to be full of Claras. Clare has, however, retained its popularity; and the French version, Claire, is fairly widely used. The name is derived from the Latin word meaning 'bright' or 'clear'. In the twelfth century, St Clare founded the order of nuns known as the Poor Clares. The name has been in use ever since, although it has remained fairly unusual. The Italian version, Chiara (pronounced Keeara) is pretty enough to be worth using if you want something really off-beat.

Clarence (m)
Name of the dukedom created for Lionel, son of Edward III. It was used for the first time as a first name in a nineteenth century novel and has appeared occasionally since, but it was never popular.

Clarice, Clarissa (f)
A French derivative of Clare, which was a name in its own right as early as the twelfth century. It occurred in one of the great medieval romances, which was enough to make it popular in the early days. Clarissa, the Latin form, enjoyed a revival after its use in an eighteenth century novel. Neither name is widely used today. The usual short form is Clarrie.

Claud(e) (m), *Claudia* (f)
Introduced to Britain from France in the sixteenth century, this was originally the name of a Roman clan. The Welsh version of the feminine form is Gwladys or Gladys. Neither masculine nor feminine versions have ever been very popular, and Claudie, the pet form of the feminine, is truly terrible. To add to the problems, the original clan name was derived from a word meaning 'lame'.

Claus (m)
See Nicholas.

Clemence, Clemency (f), *Clement* (m)
As this is derived from the Latin word meaning 'merciful', one would expect it to have been popularised with the virtue names beloved of English Puritans. In fact it has a much older tradition, although the feminine variation

Clemency probably developed in this way. The other versions are used in Britain as long ago as the thirteenth century. Clementine, a pretty nineteenth century derivation, was destroyed by the famous song about the miner and his daughter Clementine. The older versions are still used to some extent, and are attractive enough to deserve revival. Clem is the unattractive short form for the masculine version, Clemmie for the feminine.

Cleo (f)
A shortened form of Cleopatra, more adaptable to modern surnames. (I know you like the full version, madam, but Cleopatra *Jones*?) The short form means 'glory' in Greek, the full version 'father's glory'. It was originally the name of an Egyptian queen who must have been one of the most charismatic women who ever lived. Poets have always been fascinated by her, and in Shakespeare's play *Antony and Cleopatra* she receives one of the most lyrical tributes imaginable: 'Age cannot wither her, nor custom stale her infinite variety . . . ' Give your daughter this name if you are absolutely sure she can live up to it.

Cleopatra (f)
See Cleo.

Clifford (m)
Started life as a surname associated with numerous villages of this name, and has been used as a first name since the late nineteenth century. Cliff is the popular short form. It is quite popular in South Wales.

Clive (m)
Used as a Christian name in deference to Robert Clive, the great East India Company man of the eighteenth century, generally by people having family connections with India.

Clodagh (f)
A river in Ireland, borrowed as a girl's name. It suffers the disadvantage of many Irish and Welsh names – spelling and pronunciation are not phonetic by standard English criteria. It is also bound to be changed to Clogger if your

daughter grows up to be a bit beefy. Best left to the Irish, who have the tradition to treat it with respect.

Clovis (m)
See Lewis.

Colette (f)
Nowadays this pretty name is unusual in Britain and tends to be associated with the famous French novelist. Formerly it was not uncommon in this country. It is a diminutive of Nicole, the French form of Nichola. Coletta and Colet were old English variations.

Colleen (f)
This, the Irish for 'girl', was adopted in the USA as a first name and introduced from thence into Britain. It has few attractions.

Colin (m)
A commonplace modern name, with ancient lineage as a diminutive form. It started out as a French pet form of Col, itself an abbreviation of Nicholas, and appeared in thirteenth century England, but only as a nickname. It gradually died out altogether in England, but had evolved in Scotland from separate roots. In Gaelic it means 'youth' or 'young dog'. It is impossible to say whether its modern popularity throughout Britain is a revival of the French nickname or a spread of the traditional Gaelic.

Comfort (m and f)
Approach with caution this rare name, used in Britain after the Reformation. It could be a particularly hazardous choice for a girl.

Conan (m)
From Irish 'wisdom', this has never been a common name in England. Sir Arthur Conan Doyle, creator of Sherlock Holmes, was its most famous holder. It was exported from Ireland to Brittany in ancient times and was introduced to Britain from there at the time of the Norman Conquest.

Conor, Connor (m)
Another Irish name, very famous in the country's mythology. Still used, rarely, as a first name.

Conrad (m)
Although used occasionally in Britain since the fifteenth century, this is really a German name. It means 'bold counsel'.

Constance, Constantia (f)
Constance has been used in England since the Conquest. Constantia was a nineteenth century introduction of the Latin form and was viewed with disfavour as too fancy by many conventional Victorians (but then, they also regarded Edith and Alice as fancy names). Today, Constance is again the more popular form, frequently shortened to Connie. The Puritans tried to adopt it as a virtue name by modifying it to Constancy, but this was never popular. Constant has been used very occasionally as a man's name since the seventeenth century.

Constantine (m)
A Latin derivation of the word meaning 'constancy, firmness'. It has never been popular in modern times, although a variation, Costin, was used quite widely in the Middle Ages

Consuelo (f)
A Spanish name, used in this country by Roman Catholics. This name, meaning 'counsel', was originally adopted, like Mercedes and Dolores, when people felt that Mary was too sacred for everyday use. It is effectively a reverential abbreviation of Our Lady of Counsel.

Cora (f)
A nineteenth century import from the USA. It originates in the Greek word meaning 'girl'. Not popular today.

Coral (f)
A name derived from the precious substance found on

undersea reefs. It has become popular only during the present century.

Coralle (f)
French name which became popular after the Revolution and has been used occasionally in Britain. It is rather more attractive than Coral, and is probably derived from the French spelling of the word.

Cordelia (f)
This has old origins which are obscure. It certainly existed before Shakespeare adopted it for a character in *King Lear*. It is a beautiful name, but be careful about surnames. It would be difficult to find one of sufficient distinction to be suitable. Delia sometimes appears as a short form but is, in fact, a name with completely different origins.

Corinna (f)
Has a similar derivation to Cora but a much older tradition and is a far more beautiful name. Corinna is derived from the Greek word for 'maiden'. Its use by seventeenth and eighteenth century poets gave it some popularity in England but it was always unusual. The French variation, Corinne, has enjoyed some popularity in modern times, thanks to its film star associations. The English version has far more distinction. Beware of the diminutive Corrie.

Corisande (f)
A name which first appeared in medieval romance and was revived by Disraeli in the nineteenth century for one of his female characters in a novel. It is very rarely used today and its origins are obscure.

Cormac (m)
Irish name found only occasionally today as a first name, although its occurrence as a surname is more common. In Irish in means 'charioteer'.

Cornelia (f), Cornelius (m)
An ancient name derived from a Roman clan. It is rare today in both male and female forms. Has been used to anglicise

the Irish Conchubhar or Connor. In the Roman version, it was derived from the word for 'horn', and the horn signified kingship.

Cosmo (m)
Cosmo and Damian were two early Christian martyrs who became patron saints of Milan. The name Cosmo has been used occasionally by aristocratic British families. It has been fairly popular in Scotland since its introduction by the Gordon family.

Courtenay, Courtney (m)
An aristocratic surname which has been used occasionally as a first name. The first spelling is the correct one. It originated as a French place-name.

Cressida (f)
Very much a name restricted by class. It is almost unused in most social circles, but a glance through the list of debutantes at smart social functions invariably turns up one Cressida. It has no specific meaning, as it appears to be a hotch-potch of names misused and misunderstood by poets telling the tale of Troilus. The correct name of his love was Briseis, and even this was a patronymic for a girl whose personal name was Hippodamia. In the medieval romance of Troilus and Cressida, the woman became a byword for faithfulness. It is rather odd that it has been used more recently as a forename.

Crispin, Crispian (m)
A very unusual name today. A generation ago it appears to have enjoyed the same fashionable cult popularity as Gideon achieved in the 1960s. It did not so much fall from favour as simply cease to be used much. Crispin was the patron saint of shoemakers. The name means 'curled' in Latin.

Curtis (m)
Derived from the adjective 'courteous'. Curtis is more often found as a surname than as a forename. But it is used as a forename in the USA and is appearing occasionally in Britain, too. Curtiss is a modern alternative spelling.

Cuthbert (m)
An ancient name of Old English origins, derived from the words for 'famous' and 'bright'. Its popularity declined after the Middle Ages but it enjoyed a revival during the nineteenth century. During World War One it was used as a nickname for draft-dodgers, and, probably because of this, it has virtually stopped being used today.

Cynthia (f)
This name occurred from time to time in English literature but was not really popular until the late nineteenth century. It has declined again since. Cynthia was originally one of the titles of the Greek goddess Artemis. Cyn is the rather wet pet form generally used. Cynth is even worse.

Cyprian (m)
Always unusual in Britain, Cyprian enjoyed a revival in the nineteenth century. It means 'of Cyprus'. Unusual today.

Cyril (m)
Became common in Britain during the nineteenth century but has now fallen from grace. It is derived from the Greek for 'lord' or 'master'. A few years ago the phrase 'Nice one, Cyril!' was universally used in Britain as the result of its occurrence in a popular song, and promptly put the kiss of death on the name.

Cyrus (m)
The founder of the Persian Empire was called Cyrus. It means 'sun' or 'throne'. Cyrus appears in the Old Testament and thence the name was adopted by the Puritans. They took it with them to the USA, where it is still used. It is almost unknown in modern Britain. The short form, Cy, sometimes occurs.

D

Daisy (f)
This seems to be enjoying a fashionable revival among the
type of young parents who are into wholefoods, batik and
the countryside – perhaps because of its fresh, England-in-
spring image (it quite possibly lost favour among their
suburban parents thanks to its nasty-pest-in-the-lawn connotations). Daisy originated in Victorian times as a pet name
for Margaret, derived from Margeurite.

Damaris (f)
The English Puritans adopted this name, which appears in
the New Testament. The original Damaris was an Athenian
woman converted to Christianity by St Paul. It is rare today
but still occurs occasionally.

Damian (m)
One of two Greek brothers martyred in the fourth century
for their Christianity. The other was named Cosmos, or
Cosmo. Occasionally the names have been used together for
twin brothers. Damian is derived from the Greek word
meaning 'to tame'. It is extremely fashionable today, but not
commonplace.

Dandy (m)
An uncommon pet form for Andrew.

Daniel (m)
Currently very fashionable, but only in its full form. It is
Hebrew for 'God has judged'. It became rare during the
nineteenth century after centuries of popular use, but is
now right back in favour with the vogue for biblical names.
In the past it has been used to translate the Irish Domhnall
and the Welsh Deiniol. The diminutives Dan and Danny
have not shared the fashionable revival of the full version.

Daphne (f)
A Victorian authority, Charlotte Mary Yonge, is very scathing about poor Daphne in her *History of Christian Names*. She says: 'It has not been used as a name except for dogs.' But fashion overtook the name early this century and it enjoyed a burst of popularity. The original Daphne was a nymph, loved by Apollo, who turned into a laurel bush.

Darby (m)
English form of the Irish Diarmid which came to a sticky end as a forename in the *Gentleman's Magazine,* where the 'Darby and Joan' verses were first published in the eighteenth century. Ever since it has been synonymous with old age, to the extent that old people's clubs are named after the fictional pair.

D'Arcy, Darcy (m)
Originally an English surname derived from a French place name, D'Arcy was taken to Ireland where it became a first name. As such it has reappeared in England, but was never common.

Darrel, Daryl (m)
A rather unattractive name derived from the Old English word for 'darling'. From time to time it is revived, but has never been popular.

David (m)
First appeared in Britain in the form Dewi – the Welsh version. It was borne by the archbishop who became patron saint of Wales and has remained a favourite in the principality in various forms. Originally David was a Hebrew lullaby word meaning 'darling' or 'beloved'. This form was introduced to England after the Norman Conquest, and although regularly used was never particularly popular. In addition to the indigenous Welsh Dewi, David was introduced from England to Wales as Dafydd (pronounced Dahvith). Davey and Dave are the usual short forms.

Davina (f)
A feminine Scottish form of David.

Dawn (f)
A rather vulgar modern English version of the Latin Aurora. It seems to have been invented by pulp romance writers at the turn of the century, whence it was adopted for use in real life. After a brief vogue it declined, but was revived later this century due to its use by film stars.

Debbie (f)
See Deborah.

Deborah (f)
A dignified old name which has suffered many abuses from Hollywood in recent decades. Originally it was the name of a Hebrew prophetess. The name means 'a bee'. It was a favourite first name with the Puritans. Sadly, its possibilities caught the attention of the film world, and it was adapted to both Debbie and Debra. As a result, both derivations have been widely used since the 1950s. Neither version is particularly attractive, and with 'film star' names it is always worth bearing in mind that later generations can pinpoint the age of the bearer to the years of the particular star's popularity. Shirley is a good example of this.

Debra (f)
See Deborah.

Decima (f), *Decimus* (m)
From the Latin for 'tenth', much favoured for the tenth child in those enormous Victorian families. As people developed different ideas about how many children they wanted, the name gradually became redundant. Just keep your fingers crossed that you won't have need of it!

Deirdre (f)
An obscure name, originating in the romantic Celtic Revival rather than in true Celtic roots. Deirdre was the heroine of *The Sons of Uisneach*, one of the *Three Sorrowful Tales of Erinn*. Wide use of the name in modern Irish literature has made it popular. It is found quite often in England, too.

Delia (f)
Still found occasionally, Delia was most popular in the seventeenth and eighteenth centuries when it appeared in popular poetry. Originally it was an epithet for the Greek goddess Artemis, derived from Delos, her birthplace. For some odd reason, it is often used in Ireland, along with Bedelia, by women christened Bridget or Brigid.

Denis, Dennis (m), *Denise* (f)
A very popular Christian saint, the patron of France. The name is somewhat inappropriately derived from the Greek 'of Dionysos', considering the pagan associations of this name with orgiastic drinking rites. It is a commonplace modern name of little distinction. The feminine version, Denise, is adapted from the French form. The traditional English versions, Dennet, Diot and Dionis, are never found nowadays but may be worth reviving.

Denzil (m)
Originally a Cornish surname, this was first used as a forename within the family, then passed into general use. The original spelling was Denzell.

Derek, Derrick (m)
An English version of the Dutch Dirck and German Diederich, all derived from the Old German Theodoric – 'folk-ruler'. The name is still very widely used, the first spelling being more usual nowadays. The French version, Terry, is generally found in Britain only as an abbreviation of Terence or Theresa.

Dermot (m)
Anglicised version of the Irish Diarmuit, meaning 'free from envy'. Like other Celtic names, Dermot has achieved some popularity in England.

Desdemona (f)
This name might sound all right, but it is derived from the Greek for 'misery', and its most famous bearer, the Shakespearean wife of Othello, was murdered by her husband.

Apart from that, it's quite attractive! These are two fairly good reasons why the name is not used very often.

Desirée (f)
A pretty name from the French for 'desired', its one draw-back is that everyone shortens it to Dez or Dezzy, neither of which is at all desirable.

Desmond (m)
Started out as an Irish surname – it means 'man of South Munster'. Nowadays it is often found as a first name, too. It was brought to England in the late nineteenth century.

Diana, Diane (f)
The cool, elegant name of the Roman moon goddess. It has been used regularly in England since the sixteenth century, but was never common. Diane, the French version, has also gained some popularity in modern times. The Hollywood adaptation, Deanna, is deplorable.

Dilys (f)
A Welsh name now regularly used in England, too. It means 'perfect', and first appeared about a hundred years ago.

Dinah (f)
A favourite name with the working classes in nineteenth century England. In Hebrew it means 'law suit', and it was the name of a daughter of Jacob. It has been confused with Diana.

Dolores (f)
One of those names which developed as a substitute for the Virgin Mary's name, which was considered too sacred for everyday use. In this case it is a reverential Spanish abbreviation of Maria de Dolores, 'Mary of the Sorrows'. In Ireland, Catholic families sometimes translate Dolores to Dolours for a masculine forename. Dolores is sometimes used in England, and, more often, in the USA.

Dominic(k) (m)
A terribly smart name of the 1960s, now getting a bit worn. It

means 'of the Lord', and was originally given to children born on a Sunday. Until it was adopted by the trendies, Dominic was used almost exclusively by Roman Catholics.

Donald (m)
One of the most common Scottish first names, particularly in the Highlands. In Ireland the variation Donal is widespread. In modern times it has been used with increasing frequency in England. Don is the usual short form. In Gaelic it means 'world mighty'.

Donna (f)
A somewhat film star-ish name, adopted in the USA this century and now spreading to Britain. It is derived from the Italian word for 'lady'.

Dora, Dorah (f)
See Dorothy.

Dorcas (f)
Nowadays the name has an old-fashioned sound and is seldom used. In the Bible Dorcas is given as a Greek interpretation of the Aramaic Tabitha. Both names mean 'gazelle'. Dorcas was a charitable woman, saved by St Paul. The name was given to circles of women who met to do needlework for the poor.

Doreen (f)
An English version of the modern Irish Doirean, which became popular early this century. It is now too commonplace ever to be fashionable. Dorothy, the English form from which the Irish probably originated, has a prettier sound.

Dorinda (f)
Made its appearance with names like Belinda and Clarinda as a poetic conceit during the eighteenth century. This one was probably an adaptation of Dorothy. It is still used, but only rarely.

Doris (f)
Extremely unfashionable today, Doris was highly popular
with the Victorians. It was originally the name of a sea-
nymph in Greek mythology, but the British do not appear to
have used it at all until it inexplicably swept to popularity
towards the end of the nineteenth century.

Dorothea, Dorothy (f)
Dorothy and its diminutives Doll and Dolly became so
popular in England that by the eighteenth century the name
was already applied to the child's toy. Doll was also a
synonym for 'loose woman' for a while, and consequently the
name fell into disuse for a time. It originated in the Greek
words meaning 'gift of God'. Dorothy appears to have been
the earliest form in England, with Dorate a frequent variation. Dorothea became popular in the nineteenth century.
Besides Doll and Dolly, Dot, Dodo and Dodie are the usual
short forms.

Dougal (m)
Anyone who was addicted to the old *Magic Roundabout*
children's television series will have a fixed image of Dougal
as a dim, arrogant, delightful dog who whizzed around the
garden as if on wheels, and hence will be incapable of
bestowing the name on any other living creature. For those
who haven't a clue as to what I'm talking about, it's a
distinguished name with a splendidly sinister derivation.
Dougal comes from the Irish meaning 'black stranger',
which was what the Old Irish called the Norwegians who
invaded their coastline. Later it was used in Irish and Gaelic
to indicate an Englishman. Today the name is found chiefly
in the Scottish Highlands.

Douglas (m)
Started out as a Scottish surname. When adopted as a first
name it was initially bestowed on girls, and only later on
boys. Douglas derives from the Gaelic for 'dark blue', and
hence has been used widely as a river name. Nowadays it is
a popular masculine name. The awful short forms, Doug,
and, worse, Dougy, are to be avoided.

Drew (m)
A pleasing, unusual Christian name, originally the English version of the Old German Drogo – 'carry'. Although very rare today as a separate name, it is sometimes used as an abbreviation for Andrew, and as such is much pleasanter than Andy.

Drusilla (f)
Occurs very occasionally in Britain and more often in the USA. Drusilla was a Roman clan name which became popular as a first name when the Puritans adopted it, because it was used in the New Testament, not because of its Roman connotations.

Dudley (m)
One of the various aristocratic surnames which was adopted as a forename initially within the family concerned but later spread to general use. It still occurs occasionally but is unusual. The short form, Dud, sounds like a confession of failure.

Dulcie (f)
A modern name derived from the Latin word meaning 'sweet'. It does not occur before the late nineteenth century and is uncommon today.

Duncan (m)
Two early Scottish kings bore this name, but its origins are Irish. It is an adaptation of the words for 'brown warrior'. Duncan is still popular in Scotland and, in recent years, has achieved reasonable popularity in England.

Dunstan (m)
Ancient name which died out in Britain before the Reformation but was revived in the nineteenth century. It is very rare today. In Old English, Dunstan meant 'hill stone'.

Dwight (m)
Originated as an English surname. A member of the Dwight family emigrated to America during the seventeenth century

and gradually Dwight came into use there as a forename. It remains common in the USA, but is not used in Britain.

Dylan (m)
The attractive name of a legendary Welsh hero, son of the sea-god, Dylan was largely confined to Wales until the fame of the poet Dylan Thomas spread it outside the principality.

E

Eamon (m)
See Edmund.

Eartha (f)
A very uncommon name derived from the Old English eorthe, meaning 'earth'.

Easter (m and f)
Once used regularly for children of either sex born on the day of the great religious festival. It is still used occasionally, but usually following family tradition rather than date of birth. Eacy is an unusual feminine pet form.

Ebenezer (m)
Ebenezer Scrooge in Dickens's *A Christmas Carol* did not exactly improve the image of this name. It was derived from a biblical word – the name of a stone raised by Samuel to commemorate the defeat of the Philistines. It is very little used today, although the diminutive form Eben sometimes occurs in the USA.

Eden (m)
A very uncommon name which still occurs occasionally in England. It is derived from the Hebrew word meaning 'delight'.

Edgar (m)
An Old English royal name which fell out of use during the Middle Ages and was revived by the romantic poets during the nineteenth century. Edgar was the hero of *The Bride of Lammermoor*, published in 1819, and as a result the name enjoyed great popularity during the nineteenth century. It is still used, but is now less common. It derives from the Old English words meaning 'happy spear'. Sadly, it is frequently shortened to Eddie or Ed.

Edith (f)
An ancient and regal name which became somewhat debased by over-use when it was revived in the nineteenth century. It is one of those names which one now associates with ancient great-aunts rather than ancient queens. In Old English it meant 'prosperous war'. Edie is the deplorable short form.

Edmond, Edmund (m)
Another Old English name which died out and underwent the great Victorian revival, this one was not as over-exposed as some others during the nineteenth century. In Old English it means 'Rich protector'. Edmund is the correct English form. Edmond is the French version, which was sometimes used in England in the late Middle Ages.

Edna (f)
The origins of this name are obscure, but it occurs in the Apocrypha. Its popularity in nineteenth century England was probably due to its adoption as a pseudonym by a popular woman novelist. It is very unfashionable today.

Edward (m)
An overwhelmingly popular English name, frequently borne by kings. Its royal use was highly appropriate, as it is derived from the Old English meaning 'Rich guardian'. Edwards were kings of England without a break from 1272 until 1377, and since then the name's popularity appears to have had little to do with passing fashions. It is one of the very few names of purely English origin which have been adopted on the Continent. Ned and Ted are the older nicknames; Ed and Eddie are modern.

Edwin (m), *Edwina* (f)
The masculine version dates back to the sixth century but the feminine form is a modern derivation. Edwin means 'rich friend'. Its use declined after the Norman Conquest, but it was revived during the nineteenth century and has been in use ever since. Neither the masculine nor feminine form is particularly popular today.

Eglentyne (f)
A pretty Old French adaptation of the Latin name for the sweetbriar. Eglentine is an alternative spelling. It was revived in the nineteenth century after long disuse, and is used very occasionally today.

Eileen (f)
Probably an Irish development of Evelyn, although some authorities suggest that it is the Irish Helen. Aileen is an alternative spelling. Like other names with an '-een' ending (eg Maureen, Doreen), it became popular in England early this century. It is still commonplace but unfashionable. Eily, the pet form, is rather prettier than the original name.

Eithne (f)
From the Irish meaning 'little fire'. Although Eithne is the usual modern form, the traditional versions are Aine and Aithne. The name is coming back into fashion in Scotland and Ireland.

Elaine (f)
A pretty French and Welsh variation of Helen, used by Malory in his *Morte d'Arthur*, but not taken up widely as a first name in England until Tennyson re-told the tale of Lancelot and Elaine in his *Idylls of the King*. Since then it has been continuously popular, but not so much so as to become hackneyed.

Eleanor(a), *Elinor* (f)
More forms of Helen which have gained currency as separate names. Eleanor of Aquitaine introduced these versions to England when she married Henry II in the twelfth century. Alienor and Elianor have also been used. Elinor became

fashionable in the seventeenth century – Nell Gwynn's name was Elinor – but had fallen into disuse by the Victorian era. Leonora, originally a pet form, has occasionally been used as a separate name. Eleanora is the Italian version, but that, too, crops up occasionally in Britain. Nell was formally used as a short form, but today Eleanor tends to survive unabbreviated.

Eliot (m)

A first name derived from a surname which, in its turn, had developed from the earlier first name. The original was Elijah – Hebrew for 'Jehovah is God' and one of the most popular biblical names of the Middle Ages. Various surnames evolved from it, including Eliot and Ellis, and in later times these were adopted as forenames. Both derivations occur more frequently as surnames than as forenames today.

Elizabeth (f)

Elizabeth is the traditional English spelling; on the Continent it is generally Elisabeth. The name derives from the Hebrew Elisheba – 'My God is satisfaction'. First used by the Eastern Christian church, it travelled to Britain via Russia, Germany, the Low Countries and France. In the Middle Ages the French and English popular version was Isabel, Elizabeth becoming widespread by the late fifteenth century. Had it not been chosen as the name of one of England's greatest monarchs, it would probably have enjoyed little popularity in later years. There is only one English church dedicated to St Elizabeth, for instance. But Elizabeth Tudor immortalised the name. Always popular since her reign, it became positively fashionable on the accession of Queen Elizabeth II, and has remained so. There are countless pet forms, including Eliza, Betty, Bess, Bessie, Betsy, Beth, Lizzy and Liz. Today the latter is the most usual abbreviation. Continental versions of Elizabeth, and their diminutives, have also been used in this country. They include the German Elsa, Lise and Lisa; Italian Bettina; and French Elise, Lisette and Babette. Scotland has produced some pretty adaptations – Elspeth, Elspie and Elsie. Lillian started out as a pet form, but had become a separate name by the sixteenth century.

Ella (f)
Surprisingly, not a nickname, but a very old independent first name. Ella is derived from the Old German word meaning 'all'. It was already obsolete by the fourteenth century, but was revived in the nineteenth century and has been in use ever since. Ellie is not a variation, but a pet form of the name Ellen.

Ellen (f)
An early English form of Helen, long a separate name. The variations Elena, Elene, Elen and the diminutive Elot were all in use in this country until the seventeenth century. After that, they all died out and only Ellen survived. It is a very common name in Ireland.

Ellis (m)
Like Eliot, this started life as a surname derived from Elijah. It is still found chiefly as a surname, but occasionally also appears as a forename. In the seventeenth century Ellis sometimes appeared as a woman's name, but this is now thought to have been a mis-spelling of Alice.

Elma (f)
Thought to have originated as a combination of parts of Elizabeth and Mary, this name is now fairly rare in Britain, but is used frequently in the USA.

Elmer (m)
Commonplace in the USA but almost obsolete in Britain. It is derived from Aylmer.

Eloisa, Eloise (f)
See Heloise.

Elsa (f)
A German diminutive of Elizabeth. Still used, and somehow much more attractive than Elsie, the home-grown version.

Elsie, Elspeth (f)
See Elizabeth.

Eluned (f)
A Welsh name of obscure origin, it was translated into French as Linnet in the Middle Ages and this version is still used in England. Eluned survives in Wales.

Elvira (f)
Developed in Spain from German roots, Elvira means 'elf counsel'. It has been used in Britain from time to time since the nineteenth century. It is likely to be abbreviated to Vera, although the two names are unconnected.

Emmanuel (m)
A beautiful old Hebrew name meaning 'God with us'. It is seldom used outside Jewish families, possibly because it does not work well with traditional British surnames. Don't let anyone shorten it to Manny; the full version is too dignified for such treatment. Manuela and Manuelita developed as feminine forms in Spain, where a vernacular version of the masculine, Manuel, is perennially popular with gentile families. The feminine versions are encountered very rarely in England.

Emerald (f)
The name of the precious stone, adopted in modern times as a girl's forename. It seems to have come into use rather later than the Victorian and Edwardian favourites of this genre, Ruby and Pearl.

Emily, Emilia (f)
This is a Roman clan name which was used as a feminine surname in the Middle Ages by the Italian poet Boccaccio. His form was the original Latin – Emilia. Chaucer later adapted it to Emelye. It was little used until the eighteenth century, when it was mistakenly adopted as the native English form of Amelia. Emily was particularly popular in Victorian Britain, but then declined. Currently it is enjoying a revival and is right up there with the Emmas, Lucies and Charlottes. Emily has plenty of attractions. It is a pretty old British name, uncomplicated and hard to mess about. The usual short form, Em, while undistinguished, is not appalling,

and although the name is very fashionable it is certainly not commonplace.

Emlyn (*m*)
A Welsh name of obscure origin and meaning, sometimes used outside Wales.

Emma (f)
The Victorians probably invented 'smart' names, and there was much criticism of the fancy tags they dreamed up. Traditionalists wanted to stick to the plain old names which had been in use for centuries. The smart set preferred to choose from romantic literature, foreign tradition, and even the names of plants or precious stones. Ancient, obsolete names were revived and enjoyed bursts of popularity. Today we go through similar crazes, and oddly enough some of these are resurrecting the old names which went out of style for smart Victorians, adding them to our own range of fancy goods. Emma has probably been the most overworked of the modern trendy revivals of the traditional. The signs are that it has lost its cachet. Emma was to the late 1960s and early 1970s what Melanie had been to the 1950s and Samantha to the early 1960s. Sadly, it appears to be going the same way. Nobody uses Gladys, Ada, Ethel or May any more because they were so overworked at the turn of the last century. By the year 2000, everyone will be avoiding these faded fashions of the twentieth century in the same way. If you want to use Emma anyway, you may be interested to know that it was introduced to Britain before the Norman Conquest by a daughter of the Duke of Normandy who married King Ethelred the Unready and, later, King Canute. It was a medieval favourite, and the diminutive Emmot was also popular. It is derived from the Old German word meaning 'universal'.

Emmeline (f)
The origins of this name are obscure, but it appears to be connected with the German Amalie rather than the Latin Emilia. Emmeline was popular throughout the Middle Ages, then died out, to be revived in the eighteenth century. Alternative forms are Ameline, Imblen and Emblem.

Emrys (m)
See Ambrose.

Ena (f)
Became popular in England after the birth in 1887 of Princess Ena, later Queen of Spain. It is used in Ireland as a part-anglicised version of Eithne. Use of the name for the hairnet-clad Ena Sharples in the popular television series *Coronation Street* probably killed any chance it had of fashionable revival.

Enid (f)
A Welsh name which became fashionable in England after the publication of the tale of Geraint and Enid in Tennyson's *Idylls of the King*. It is possibly derived from the Welsh word meaning 'tree bark'.

Enoch (m)
One of the biblical names beloved by the Puritans. It has not been part of the current revival of such names. In Hebrew, Enoch means 'trained' or 'skilled'. It is rare nowadays, the best-known holder being the politician Enoch Powell.

Ephraim (m)
Still current in the USA, Ephraim is virtually obsolete in Britain. It is a pleasant name, and would be worth reviving were it not for the unattractive short form, Eph. Ephraim means 'meadow' in Hebrew, and the biblical Ephraim was the second son of Joseph.

Eric (m), *Erica* (f)
Achieved renewed popularity in Victorian times after centuries of disuse thanks to Dean Farrar's moral tale *Eric: or Little by Little*. Originally Eric was introduced to Britain by the Danes. Its probable meaning is 'eternal ruler'. Although still widely used, it has a somewhat prissy sound, possibly because of its moral tale connotations. In fact the Eric in the story slipped down the primrose path to destruction. Erica, the feminine form, appears to have been invented in the 1880s. Both are sometimes found in Britain in their Scandinavian forms, Erik and Erika.

Ermyntrude (f)
Anyone who has followed the dotty progress of the television series *Magic Roundabout* over the past few years will know that this is a delightful name – for an aristocratic cow. The name is derived from the Old German meaning 'universal strength'. It has been obsolete in England for a long time – unless you have a distinguished cow who needs a name, of course!

Ernest (m), *Ernestine* (f)
Ernest was very popular with the Victorians, probably because it means just what it appears to mean, and earnest-ness was a much-admired quality during the nineteenth century. It received a boost when Oscar Wilde used it for the name of his hero in the play *The Importance of Being Earnest*, about a young man who had been abandoned in a handbag as a baby. It is not popular today. The common abbreviation is Ernie, and this name was adopted in the 1950s for the Electronic Random Number Indicating Equip-ment which selects the winning numbers of premium savings bonds. Ernestine, the feminine form, was coined during the nineteenth century and was never as widely used as Ernest. Tina is the usual short form.

Errol (m)
The meaning of this name is obscure but it possibly derives from Eral, a medieval form of Harold. There is a Welsh version, Eryl, which is still quite popular in Wales, but it appears to have different roots from Errol. The latter had an undesirably movie-starrish image, thanks to Errol Flynn, who buckled many a swash during the 1940s and 1950s.

Esmé (m and f)
Introduced to Britain through Scotland, where it was used by a Duke of Lennox during the sixteenth century and there-after adopted by the Stuarts as a family first name. It appears to have originated as a mis-spelling of the French Aime – the Duke's mother was French. Other Scottish families took up the name, and later it spread to England. In the nineteenth century it began to be used as a girl's name, probably from

77

confusion with Ismay, and today it is found more frequently as a feminine name than as a masculine one.

Esmeralda (f)
Occasionally used as a Christian name in England since it featured in Victor Hugo's *The Hunchback of Notre Dame*. Esmeralda is the Spanish word for 'emerald'.

Esmond (m)
Derived from an Old English word meaning 'grace' and 'protection', Esmond died out as a first name in the fourteenth century, but re-appeared after Thackeray had used it for a character's surname in a nineteenth century novel.

Estelle, Estella (f)
Direct adaptation of the French etoile – 'star', Estelle became popular in Britain after Dickens used a variation for the heroine of *Great Expectations*. There is a pretty Spanish version, Estrella (pronounced Estrellya) which sometimes appears in Britain. Estelle and Estella are uncommon today, and Stella, which means the same but developed separately, is more popular.

Esther (f)
Among the best of the Old Testament names, traditionally used in Jewish families and increasingly popular with gentiles, it appears to derive from an old Persian word meaning 'myrtle'. It did not appear in England before the seventeenth century. Initially Hester and Esther were freely interchangeable, but developed later as separate names. Hetty is the old fashioned pet name for Hester.

Ethan (m)
Ethan Allen was a hero of the American Revolution, so his name has been used frequently in the USA and is still popular. It is very rare in Britain. Ethan is Hebrew for 'perennial', referring to the streams that flow all the year round. It was originally adopted in English-speaking countries because it appears in the Bible.

Ethel (f)
Started life as a pet form of the rather formidable range of
Old English names which includes Ethelburga, Ethelinda
and Ethelfleda. It was not used before the nineteenth century
as a separate name. Ethel means 'noble'. Unfortunately,
the Victorians made too much of it, and the Edwardians
overused it too. Now it has joined the ranks of Ada, Gladys
and Maud as the eternal great-aunt name. Possibly it will be
rediscovered, along with the others, and soar to fashion again
in a couple of generations, but its time is not yet.

Etta (f)
See Henrietta.

Eugene (m) *Eugenia, Eugénie* (f)
The masculine form is encountered only rarely in Britain.
In America it is more popular, usually appearing in the
shortened form Gene. It derives from the Greek word meaning 'noble'. Eugenia is the traditional feminine form in
Britain, but is not as pretty as Eugénie, which was made
fashionable in France by the Empress Eugénie in the nineteenth century and spread to this country. Both feminine
versions are unusual.

Eulalia, Eulalie (f)
It means 'sweet speaking' in Greek, and would be a lovely
name – except that its sounds conjures up the word
'ululate', producing an image of someone howling gently. If
it doesn't affect you in this way, go ahead and use it; but be
prepared for people to call her Lally.

Eunice (f)
A name which, on the lips of the inexperienced, can make
lovers of classical pronunciation wince. It is correctly pronounced Unissay, not Uniss, which is the usual modern
method. Eunice means 'happy victory' in Greek. It was
adopted by the Puritans in the seventeenth century because it
appeared in the New Testament. Uncommon today, but still
used.

Eustace (m) *Eustacia* (f)
Not used often nowadays, possibly because of its use for the
cartoon character Useless Eustace. It means 'fruitful', and
its origins are Greek. The feminine form Eustacia developed
during the nineteenth century. Until then both men and
women were called Eustace.

Eva, Eve (f)
From the Hebrew word 'lively', this is accepted as the biblical name of the first woman, although the Jews do not appear
to have used it. Eve, the native English version, is prettier
than the Latin Eva. The Gaelic Aoiffe, used in Scotland and
Ireland, has been rendered as Eve. It seems to be one of
those names to which people keep adding suffixes, hence the
pet form Evie.

Evadne (f)
A Greek name of obscure meaning. It is used from time to
time as a modern forename, but is difficult to blend with
British surnames.

Evan (*m*)
A partially anglicised Welsh version of John. The correct
Welsh spelling would be Ifan.

Evangeline (f)
A rather musical name, derived from the Greek for 'bringer
of good tidings', but used as a name only in modern times. It
was invented by Longfellow for the heroine of the poem of
that name.

Evelina (f), *Evelyn* (m and f)
Originally Evelyn evolved purely as a girl's name, but was
adopted as a boy's name too from the surname Evelyn which
existed in the seventeenth century. It derives from the Old
German name Avi. Evelina is the Latin form, and has been
largely displaced by Evelyn. An old and pretty variation is
Aveline, but this appears to have been obsolete since the
early nineteenth century.

Everard (m)
Everard is usually found today as a surname, but occasionally appears as a first name. It originated in the Old German meaning 'hard boar'.

Ewan, Ewen, Euan (m)
Now confined largely to Scotland and North-East England, Ewan was once common throughout the country. It is derived from the Irish and Gaelic words for 'youth'.

Ezekiel (m)
About the only place you are likely to encounter an Ezekiel these days is in old Western movies – and then they'll all call him Zeke! It means 'may God strengthen' in Hebrew.

Ezra (m)
Became popular in seventeenth century England and lasted until early this century. It now appears to be obsolete. In Hebrew, Ezra means 'help'.

F

Fabian (m)
Rarely used today, this originated as a Roman clan name. Fabian has also appeared as a surname.

Faith (f)
One of the virtue names beloved by English Puritans during the seventeenth century. Female triplets were often called Faith, Hope and Charity, presumably to ensure that no one ignored the family's virtue. It is fairly unusual today.

Fanny (f)
See Frances.

Farquhar (m)
From the Gaelic meaning 'friendly man'. It is still used in Scotland but has never been popular elsewhere.

Fay (f)
A pretty modern name of obscure origin. It could be an abbreviation of Faith, or possibly the word fay meaning 'fairy'.

Felicia (f)
Fore-runner of the more modern Felicity, Felicia has a similar derivation – from the Latin word for 'happiness'. The early version in England was Felice, which has led to frequent confusion with Phyllis. Today Felicity is far more widely used. Both are pretty, unusual names and are difficult to abbreviate.

Felicity (f)
See Felicia.

Felix (m)
Rare masculine form of Felicia and Felicity.

Fenella (f)
A novel by Sir Walter Scott gave this name a passing vogue during the nineteenth century but it has never been popular. It is derived from the Irish Fionnghuala – 'white shoulder'. Fenella is still used occasionally in England, but in Ireland the usual form is Finola.

Ferdinand (m)
A German name which was enthusiastically adopted in Spain. It derives from the Old German words for 'voyage' and 'risk'. Ferdinand was regularly used in England until the seventeenth and eighteenth centuries, when the Italian version, Ferdinando, suddenly became popular. It still occurs in this country, but once more the native form has replaced the Italian. It is rather fancy for today's surnames, and the abbreviation, Ferdie, is awful, two possible reasons for its present unpopularity.

Fergus (m)
Only occasionally found outside Scotland and Ireland. In Old Irish it is a combination of the words for 'man' and 'choice'.

Finola (f)
See Fenella.

Fiona (f)
Although this has a 'traditional Gaelic' sound, it is a relatively modern invention, apparently devised by William Sharp in the nineteenth century for his *nom de plume* Fiona Macleod. In Gaelic fionn means 'fair' or 'white', and it is presumably derived from this. Fiona is still fairly popular.

Fleur (f)
Few recently-invented forenames can be as pretty as this. The writer John Galsworthy coined it for his beautiful, headstrong heroine, Fleur Forsyte. It is a direct adoption of the French word for 'flower'. Fleur is still used occasionally, and enjoyed a burst of popularity when *The Forsyte Saga* was adapted for television.

Flora (f)
Flora has enjoyed continuous popularity in Scotland since it was introduced there from France. Nowadays it is used in England, too, but it used to be considered suitable for dogs rather than women. The original Flora was the Roman goddess of flowers.

Florence (f)
A rare name until Florence Nightingale turned it into a craze in the nineteenth century. It is derived from the Latin word meaning 'blooming'. The many short forms are all pretty awful, for example, Flo, Florrie and Flossie, and are the probable reasons for the name falling from favour.

Flower (f)
Quite simply, this means what it says. Never commonplace and not as pretty as Fleur.

Frances (f), *Francis* (m)
Frances came into use in Britain far later than in other
countries. It is not found before the sixteenth century, and
the masculine version, Francis, appeared only a little earlier.
Both names are derived from the Latin term for 'French-
man'. The name enjoyed great popularity on the Continent
from an early date in deference to St Francis of Assissi. The
short form Frank originally applied to girls as well as boys.
It endured as a masculine nickname, while Fran, Fanny
and, later, Frankie, took over for girls. The Italian feminine
form, Francesca, has been used occasionally in this country
during the twentieth century.

Frank (m)
A common abbreviation for Francis which became a
separate name quite early. In fact it was known in England
before the introduction here of Francis, as a name represent-
ing the Old German Franco, 'a Frank'.

Freda (f)
See Winifred.

Frederic(*k*) (m), *Frederica* (f)
Until the seventeenth century the English tended to use a
French name, Frery or Fery, rather than Frederic. It became
really common when the Hanoverian dynasty took over the
British throne and introduced it from Germany. As a really
commonplace name, its heyday was over by the early years
of the present century. There were simply too many Freds
about for it to last. Frederick is the usual modern spelling.
It is still quite common, but unfashionable. The name was
originally Old German, and meant 'peace-ruler'. Frederica,
the feminine form, is a nineteenth century invention. Fred
and Freddie are the common short forms.

G

Gabriel (m), *Gabrielle* (f)
The rarely-used name of the Archangel of the Annunciation.
In Hebrew it means 'God is a strong man', or 'strong man of
God'. The original feminine form was Gabriela, from the
Latin, but in modern times the French version has taken
over. Gabby is the unfortunate short form.

Gail (f)
See Abigail.

Galahad (m)
A very glamorous name, but not suitable for modern times.
Galahad was the spotless knight, son of Sir Lancelot, who
alone succeeded in the quest for the Holy Grail. In other
words, he was simply too good to be true. His character is
summed up in the popular Victorian poem about his
prowess:

> My good blade carves the casques of men,
> My strong lance thrusteth sure;
> My strength is as the strength of ten
> Because my heart is pure . . .

If you want an Arthurian name, it might be wiser to stick
to Gareth or Kay.

Gareth (m)
A corruption of the Welsh word for 'gentle', Gareth is a
fairly rare name, more often encountered in Wales than
elsewhere. It was borne by one of King Arthur's knights,
and was drawn to popular attention in the nineteenth century in Tennyson's *Gareth and Lynette*. Gary and Garth are
modern forms, and sound like it.

Garfield (m)
A rare name derived from the Old English 'spear field'.

Gavin (m)
See Gawain.

Gawain (m)
One of King Arthur's best-known knights in the legends. The Welsh origin of the name derives from the words meaning 'white hawk'. There is a separate tradition which developed from German roots and culminated in the French variation Gavin. Nowadays Gavin, once popular only in Scotland, is a favourite of the trendies. It is a very attractive name and does not shorten easily – Gav somehow sounds unconvincing. Gawain itself is quite rare today.

Gay (f)
A modern adoption of the English adjective as a girl's name. Over the past decade it has developed somewhat equivocal associations, so if you must choose it, it might be better to spell it Gaye.

Gaynor (f)
See Guenevere.

Gemma (f)
Italian word for 'gem' which, surprisingly, was used as a girl's name as early as the thirteenth century. It appears occasionally today.

Gene (m)
See Eugene.

Genevieve (f)
An elegant name of French origin which has been adopted in England too. The meaning is obscure, although it is known to have Old German origins. It is particularly popular in France because of the tradition that St Genevieve saved Paris from the Huns in the fifteenth century. As a result she is patron saint of the city.

Geoffrey, Jeffrey (m)
Geoffrey is the older version of this name. The meaning is obscure, but it is thought to derive from the Old German

'peace pledge'. Jeffrey is a comparatively modern version. Geoff or Jeff are the usual short forms. It is very widely used today, although not particularly fashionable.

George (m)
A solid, reliable old name, as English as roast beef and Yorkshire pudding – except that it was originally Greek and even today it is one of the most popular Greek masculine names. It means 'farmer' or 'tiller of the soil'. The cult of St George, who was a Roman legionary, killed in Nicomedia in the fourth century, was brought to Britain by Crusaders returning home from the East. Although he was adopted as patron saint of England in the fourteenth century, his name did not become popular until the Hanoverians made George the monarch's name for more than a century. As a result, it is regarded today as being characteristically English – except by the Greeks, of course. Georgie is the usual pet name everywhere but north-eastern England, where Geordie is so universally used that it has become the standard nickname for a man from that part of the country.

Georgia, Georgiana, Georgina (f)
Feminine versions of George, all coined when the Hanoverians popularised the masculine form. Georgiana is probably the most attractive, Georgina the version most obviously a straightforward adaptation of a man's name. Try to avoid the use of the unisex short form, Georgie. Otherwise, the feminine variations are all good choices.

Geraint (m)
An old Welsh name still very popular in Wales and occasionally used elsewhere, it is probably derived from the Greek word meaning 'old'. In England it is sometimes pronounced Jeraint, but this is not correct. The G should be hard, and the second syllable should be 'ant', not 'aynt'. The name was popularised to some extent outside Wales when Tennyson retold the story of Geraint and Enid in his *Idylls of the King*.

Gerald (m), Geraldine (f)
Originally Gerald was far less commonplace than the similar

Gerard, with which it was frequently confused. Gerald virtually died out in the thirteenth century but suddenly became popular again at the end of the Victorian era, It has remained so, and although not fashionable, appears to be a fixture. It is quite pleasant if you can prevent use of the short form Gerry, which is appalling. Geraldine seems to have been invented by the poet Surrey, who used it to describe a woman of the Fitzgerald family in the sixteenth century. It was picked up as a feminine name early in the nineteenth century and has been used ever since. It is quite commonplace today.

Gerard (m)
Originally more common than the similar Gerald, Gerard has now become the unusual name. It is derived from the Old German 'hard spear'. It is distinguished and adapts well to various surnames. Use it if you like Gerald but want something less mundane. There is an Irish version, Garret, which is still in use.

Gerda (f)
Purely a Scandinavian name until relatively modern times, when the popularity of the Hans Andersen story *The Snow Queen* brought it to popular notice in this country. Now it appears here occasionally.

Gertrude (f)
However much you love your great-aunt Gert, that awful and universal short form is bound to put you off the name. In Norse mythology, one of the Valkyries was called Gertrude – it means 'spear strength'. It has a hard, uncompromising sound, suitable for one of the female warriors who carried dead heroes from the battlefields to bliss in Valhalla, the Norse heaven. Nowadays it sounds dated, probably because it was very popular during the nineteenth century. The only pretty thing about it is the pet form, Trudie or Trudy, which in recent years has become an independent first name.

Gervase (m)
Old German name meaning 'spear vassal' which has now

virtually died out as a forename. It survives as a surname in Jarvis, which is also used from time to time as a first name.

Gideon (m)
Ultra-fashionable in modern times, the name the smart columnists always ascribe to sophisticated young men who enjoy fast cars and faster girls. In the Old Testament story, Gideon routed the Midianite hordes with only three hundred men. It was adopted in Britain during the sixteenth century, when Huguenot refugees introduced it from France.

Gilbert (m)
Nowadays rather dated, though the short form Gil can sound smart enough in its way. The name has an attractive meaning in Old German – 'bright pledge'. It has always been popular in Scotland, probably because it was used to render the Gaelic Gilbride ('servant of St Bridget').

Giles (m)
Giles was the patron saint of cripples and beggars. Originally it appeared as a woman's name as well as a man's, but today only the masculine form is used. The name derives from the Greek word meaning 'kid'. It is unusual enough to be interesting without being outrageously so. It is almost impossible to shorten and adapts to practically any surname.

Gillian (f)
Started life as a popular English version of Julian. In the Middle Ages the short forms Gill, Jill, Gillot and Gillet were very common. After a decline, it has been revived in the twentieth century, in its full form and as the separate name Jill. Jilly is a modern pet form. In earlier times, the short form Jillet became a synonym for flightiness, and eventually evolved into the word 'jilt'.

Ginevra (f)
See Guenevere.

Gisela (f)
This is the original British version of an Old German name

meaning pledge. It is still used in this country, but the French version, Gisele, is now more popular. Even this form is fairly unusual.

Gladys (f)
Gladys has such an outmoded image these days that it is hard to believe it was the name of a great beauty of the age – Gladys Cooper – earlier this century. It has lost its glamour, probably because it is another name which was overworked by the Victorians and Edwardians. Gladys is derived from the Welsh name Gwladys, itself a vernacular version of the Latin Claudia.

Gloria (f)
It's a nice idea to call your daughter by a name adapted from the Latin 'glory', but somehow it doesn't work. Possibly too many film stars were called Gloria.

Godfrey (m)
A traditional English name nowadays found most often as a surname. The medieval Godfrey was introduced to Britain from Normandy, but its origins were Old German, deriving from the words meaning 'God's peace'.

Godwin (m)
One of the most common Old English names, Godwin had some illustrious bearers, including the Earl of Mercia who fathered Harold Godwinson, the last Saxon king of England. The name means 'good friend'. It is unusual as a first name today, and is distinguished enough to deserve revival.

Gordon (m)
Originally a Scottish family name, it became enormously popular as a forename thanks to the fame of General Gordon in the nineteenth century. It is no longer fashionable, but is still widely used.

Goronwy (m)
Still used in Wales, this Christian name suffers considerably

from its hideous and universally-used abbreviation – Gron. Its meaning and origins are obscure.

Grace (f)
This means grace in the old, religious sense of the word, not gracefulness. It was adopted as a forename by the Puritans, along with the other virtues. The heroic Grace Darling, who captured the public imagination during the nineteenth century, made the name enormously popular. It is still widely used. The pet form Gracie is sometimes given as a separate name.

Graham(e) (m)
Another Scottish surname which became a forename in modern times. It is quite popular and is worth choosing if you want something which does not lend itself to short forms.

Grainne (f)
A popular Irish name sometimes rendered in English as Grace. Not common outside Ireland.

Gregory (m)
Everyone will call him Greg, so you may as well save time and name him that in the first place. Gregory is a very distinguished name, but it simply never gets left alone. It is derived from the Greek meaning 'watchman'. Several popes bore the name, and as a result it fell out of favour after the Reformation. Gregour was the medieval English form, which evolved as the popular Gregor in Scotland and later formed the surname McGregor.

Greta (f)
The popularity of the film actress Greta Garbo in the 1930s led to a passing vogue for this name. It is the Swedish abbreviation of Margaret.

Gretel, Gretchen (f)
Like Greta, these are foreign abbreviations of Margaret which have been used from time to time in Britain. These two are German.

Guendolen, Gwendolyn (f)
The Gwendolyns of legend seem to have been enchantresses: one was a fairy with whom King Arthur fell in love; the other married Merlin, the magician. The name appears to be associated with the ancient Celtic moon goddess. It derives from the words meaning 'white circle'. Gwen and Gwenda, the modern short forms, are now used more often than the full name.

Guenevere, Guinevere (f)
A beautiful, regal name which sounds more attractive than the original Welsh form, Gwenhwyfar (pronounced Gwen-high-var). The modern Gaynor and Jennifer are derived from it, but neither has the grace and dignity of the original. It is often abbreviated to Jenny, which, although pretty, is not up to the full version. The best-known Guinevere was the wife of King Arthur.

Guy (m)
Terse, uncompromising, impossible to shorten; it's a good name for a tough little boy, or for any other sort of little boy for that matter. Its meaning is unknown, but it originated in Germany. Guy Fawkes's unfortunate behaviour drove it out of fashion for two hundred years, but it was revived in the nineteenth century and has been used regularly ever since.

Gwen(da) (f)
See Guendolen.

Gwyneth (f)
A popular Welsh name, now used in England too. It means 'blessed'. Gwyn is the pet form.

H

Hamish (m)
Believe it or not, this is a Gaelic rendering of James! In fact,
it is somewhat phoney. The true Gaelic form is Sheumais or
Seamus; Hamish is an attempt to render it phonetically.

Hannah (f)
The Greek form of this Hebrew name developed as Ann, but
Hannah was introduced to England separately during the
seventeenth century. In Hebrew the name means 'God has
favoured me'. It is far less commonplace than Ann and its
variations, and is a pleasant, dignified name with a long
tradition. Like Ann, it suffers from the short form Annie.
It has enjoyed a minor vogue in the late 1970s.

Harold (m)
Originally a German name which was introduced to Anglo-
Saxon England by the Vikings, in the Scandinavian form,
Harald. It fell from grace after Harold Godwinson, successor
to Edward the Confessor, lost the English crown to William
of Normandy. It was revived, as Harold, during the nineteenth century, and has survived in that form to the present
day. It is somewhat undistinguished and, although still widely
used, not fashionable. Harry is the usual short form. It means
'army power'.

Harriet (f)
A stylish British version of the French Henriette – a feminine
form of Henry. Originally imported to England by Charles I's
queen, Henriette Marie, it was usually latinised as Henrietta
for the christening but in normal use was Harriet, just as
Henry becomes Harry. Hatty is the usual short form, but try
to avoid it. It is totally at variance with the stately Harriet.
The original form, Henrietta, appears to be virtually obsolete
today.

Harry (m)
See Henry.

Hartley (m)
Started life as a surname derived from a placename. Hartley is occasionally used as a forename today.

Harvey (m)
Although, like Hartley, this is found most often as a surname today, it was originally a first name, derived from the French Herve and introduced to England by the Normans. It means 'battle-worthy' in Old French. Harvey is still used quite often as a Christian name in the USA, but is much rarer in Britain.

Hatty (f)
See Harriet.

Hazel (f)
Adopted directly from the plant name in the vogue for plant and flower names which developed during the nineteenth century. Still used, but rather undistinguished.

Heather (f)
Like Hazel, a plant name adopted as a girl's name in the nineteenth century. More popular in Scotland than elsewhere.

Hebe (f)
Hebe was the Greek goddess of youth, cupbearer to the gods. The name literally means 'youth'. It crops up very occasionally as a Christian name in Britain.

Hector (m)
For some reason, possibly because it was used to render a Gaelic name, Hector took root in Scotland and has remained popular there. It originated in Greece, and was the name of the son of Priam, king of Troy in Homer's epic *The Iliad*. Hector means 'hold fast'.

Helen (f)

One of the classic women's names, along with a very few others like Sarah and Elizabeth. It has been so popular, and in so many countries, that today a seemingly infinite variety of independent names exist which started out as simple variations of Helen. Eleanor, Ellen, Elaine and Leonora are just a few examples. Helen originated in Greece and means 'bright one'. It became universally popular in reverence to St Helena, daughter of a British king and mother of the Roman Emperor Constantine, who is said to have discovered the True Cross. It appears impervious to changes of fashion, and never suffered the devaluation which results from over-use. Nell, the only short form, is little used today. Choose Helen if you want something distinguished, traditional and dignified which will combine happily with almost any modern surname.

Helewise (f)

Introduced to England by the Normans in the French form Heloise. The most famous bearer of this name was the heroine of one of the great – true – medieval romantic tales, about an aristocratic girl who fell in love with the monk who was her tutor. The English version of the name, Helewise, sounds somewhat clumsy in comparison with Heloise, and when it was revived in the eighteenth century it appeared as an evolved form of the latter, Eloise or Eloisa. The middle vowels are pronounced as separate sounds, making the correct pronunciation Elo-eez, not Eloyce. The name has some distinction in this form, and is occasionally used today. If you choose it, make sure that it is pronounced properly, as the incorrect pronunciation gives rise to the ghastly short form, Loisie.

Helga (f)

A Norse name, still widely used in Scandinavia. It means 'holy'. It was used in Britain until about the time of the Norman Conquest, probably as a result of the strong Scandinavian influence here at the time, but died out fairly early. The name was taken to the USA and has spread thence to Britain in modern times. It is not often used.

Henrietta (f), *Henry* (m)

The masculine form, always popular in Britain, has enjoyed a revival in recent years along with other simple, traditional names like William and Thomas. Henry is derived from the Old German words meaning 'home ruler', and just about every European country has a national version. In Germany it is Heinrich or Heinz; in Scandinavia Henrik; in the Netherlands Hendrik; in France Henri; in Italy Enrico and in Spain Enrique. The British seem incapable of leaving any name in its proper form and Henry quickly became Harry. Harry it remained, until it declined during the first half of this century. Now that it is back in fashion, Harry is frowned on. It may still be used, but Henry is the smart version. Henrietta developed from the French feminine form, Henriette. It was introduced to England by Charles I's French queen, Henriette Marie. Her name was anglicised as Henrietta Maria. Harriet developed early as a feminine diminutive in the same way that Harry developed from Henry. In this case, however, Harriet has remained a more fashionable form. Henrietta is quite unusual today.

Hephzibah (f)

Hebrew name with a lovely meaning – 'my delight is in her'. Unfortunately, it does not match well with non-Jewish surnames, and, possibly for this reason, is almost unused by gentile families in Britain. At the turn of the century Hepsie was recorded as a shortened version, but appears not to have been used since.

Herbert (m)

This has an oddly dated sound, possibly because it enjoyed a popular revival at the end of the nineteenth century and there are still a lot of elderly Herberts around as a result. The name is of Old German origin and means 'bright army'. Bert, Bertie, Herb and Herbie have all been used as short forms for Herbert.

Hercules (m)

There are some Greek names which work in modern use and some which do not. Hercules definitely doesn't, possibly because it is impossible to imagine this synonym for primitive strength and power linked with a surname. Its only notable use in recent years has been as the name of a rag-and-bone merchant's horse in the television series *Steptoe and Son*.

Hereward (m)
If you have a fairly aristocratic surname and are itching to impress everyone, here is the perfect name. Hereward was the Old English hero who resisted the Normans in Britain after 1066, a sort of real-life Robin Hood. The name was revived by Charles Kingsley in 1866 in his novel *Hereward the Wake*, which retold the old stories. Hereward has been used very occasionally since then. It is derived from the Old English meaning 'army guard'.

Hermia (f)
See Hermione.

Hermione (f)
Two glorious theatrical grandes dames, Hermione Gingold and Hermione Baddeley, have bestowed a tinge of eccentric glamour on this name. Of Greek origins, it means 'daughter of Hermes'. Hermione has been used in modern times largely because Shakespeare chose it for a character in *A Winter's Tale*. Another version, Hermia, has been used for much the same reason, because it is the name of a character in *A Midsummer Night's Dream*.

Hero (f)
It's surprising how many people imagine that this is a man's name, not a girl's, presumably because courageous men are known as heroes. The name is nothing to do with the noun. Its meaning is obscure, although it is known to have originated in Greece. Hero was the Greek beauty for whom Leander swam to his death. It is distinctive and unusual, but if you choose it, be prepared for your daughter to suffer a certain amount of teasing.

Hester, Hetty (f)
See Esther.

Hilary (m and f)
The name comes from the Latin Hilarius – 'cheerful' improbable though this may seem. Today it is used primarily as a woman's name, but until this century it was almost exclusively masculine. Hillary is an alternative spelling of the masculine version. The name has a lot to recommend it; simplicity, dignity and long tradition. Beware the short form Hilly.

Hilda (f)
An Old English name meaning 'battle', Hilda has been used in England since Anglo-Saxon times. Like many names which became fashionable again in Victorian days, it sounds somewhat dated today.

Hiram (m)
A biblical name which became popular in England during the seventeenth century and was introduced to North America by the Puritans. Hiram is still fairly popular in the USA but is probably obsolete in Britain. It means 'exalted brother', and was the name of a king of Tyre.

Honor(ia) (f)
An old name which was very popular with the Anglo-Normans during the Middle Ages, and revived by the Puritans as a 'virtue' name. In Latin it means 'reputation' or 'honour'. In Ireland it became Nora, which was then reintroduced to England as a separate name. Annora was an early variation in England, now uncommon.

Hope (f)
Became popular with the Puritans, along with all the other virtue names in the seventeenth century. Triplets were frequently christened Faith, Hope and Charity. Hope was originally used for either sex, but quickly became exclusively feminine.

Horace, Horatio (m)
Both are out of fashion at present. Horatio spread to England from Italy during the sixteenth century. It originated as a clan name in ancient Rome. Horatio achieved a

certain popularity thanks to the fame of Admiral Lord Nelson. Horace developed as the usual form in Britain.

Howard (f)
An aristocratic surname which was adopted as a forename by people unconnected with the great families, and passed into general use. The surname itself appears to have originated as Hayward. The hayward was the medieval manor official entrusted with the hay crop.

Howell (m)
An anglicised version of the Welsh Hywel (which is pronounced in the same way as Howell). In Welsh it means 'famous'.

Hubert (m)
Another example of an ancient name revived during the nineteenth century, overused and consequently seldom encountered today. Hubert developed from the Old German Hugubert – 'bright heart'.

Hugh, Hugo (m)
Hugo is the Latin version, Hugh the Anglo-Norman, introduced to Britain after the Conquest as Hugues. It originated in an Old German word meaning 'heart' or 'soul'. Hugh became very popular, partly because of its association with St Hugh of Lincoln. It was used in Scotland and Ireland to anglicise various Gaelic names. Huw is a native Welsh version, pronounced in the same way as Hugh. All forms are fairly popular today, with Hugo having a slightly aristocratic edge over the others.

Humphrey (m)
A lordly name of Old German origin, introduced to Britain by the Normans. It means 'peace giant'. Through the ages it became extremely popular, so much so that in 1863 Charlotte Mary Yonge wrote in her *History of Christian Names:* 'From being a noble and knightly name, Humphrey, as we barbarously spell it, came to be a peasant's appellation, and is now almost disused.' (The original French spelling

used an f instead of ph). Humphrey recovered some of its status later in the nineteenth century, although it is not widely used today.

I

Iain, Ian (m)
Gaelic versions of John, now used in England and Wales, as well as Scotland. Iain is the authentic spelling, Ian a later variation.

Ida (f)
An old English name which has suffered eclipse in recent years because a nineteenth century revival resulted in overuse. It is derived from German roots, and means 'work'. Ida was introduced to Britain by the Normans. It is an attractive name, worth considering for its simplicity as much as anything. Ida is another of those too rare names which cannot be messed about easily.

Idonea (f)
Although this rare name has a vaguely italianate sound, it is of Norse origins. It started life as Iduna, the name of the Norse goddess of spring.

Idris (m)
A popular Welsh name, meaning, romantically, 'fire lord'. The only snag is that people tend to shorten it to Id – neither fiery nor lordly. The Welsh mountain, Cader Idris (Idris's Chair), was, according to legend, the observatory of a giant called Idris who was a great astronomer and magician.

Ifor (m)
See Ivor.

Ignatius (m)
A Latin name of obscure origin, generally found in Britain
only among Roman Catholics.

Igor (m)
A Russian name of Scandinavian origin, sometimes used in
this country in the past. It is unlikely to survive this generation, as it appears to have become a favourite name for the
mad assistant in Frankenstein movies.

Ilona (f)
A rare, lovely name of Hungarian origin, occasionally found
in Britain. It means 'beautiful one', and is possibly a derivation of Helen.

Imogen (f)
Originated as a mis-spelling of Innogen, the heroine of
Shakespeare's play *Cymbeline*. Imogen survived, and during
the past century or so it has been used as a first name. It is
very pretty and unusual enough to become fashionable in
the future. The correctly-spelled Innogen appears to derive
from the Greek for 'beloved child'.

Inez (f)
A Spanish form of Agnes.

Ingram (m)
More generally found today as a surname than as a forename, Ingram is distinguished and attractive enough for
revival. The name, derived from Old English, means 'dark
angel'.

Ingrid (f)
An old Norse name meaning 'heroic ride'. It died out in
medieval England, but in modern times has been reintroduced from Scandinavia.

Inigo (m)
A home-grown British version of Ignatius, now virtually
obsolete.

101

Iola (f)
Comparatively rare in Britain, Iola means 'dawn cloud' in Greek.

Iona (f)
Adapted as a girl's name from the Hebridean island. It originated as the Greek word to describe a violet-coloured stone. Seldom found outside Scotland.

Irene (f)
A beautiful name, but *do* pronounce it properly. It should have three syllables – Ireenee – not two. The Americans invented the 'Ireen' pronunciation, which has now spread to Britain. The name means 'peace' in Greek. It was not used in Britain before the late nineteenth century. As if the two-syllable pronunciation were not damaging enough, Irene is frequently shortened to Renie.

Iris (f)
Not one of the flower-names which became popular in the nineteenth century, Iris is Greek for 'rainbow', and this is the true derivation of it as a girl's name. It comes from a delightful Greek myth – Iris carried messages to men from the gods, using the rainbow as a bridge. It is another of the names which were so popular during the Victorian era that they are now out of favour, at least temporarily.

Isaac (m)
A Hebrew name which was common in England after the Reformation, but has now virtually died out. It means 'God may laugh', and was the name of the son of Abraham and Sarah. During the seventeenth century it was frequently spelled Izaak.

Isabel(la), *Isobel* (f)
Originally this was a variation of Elizabeth, which developed in the South of France and became a separate name quite early in history. Isabel was the name of three medieval queens of England, which may explain why the form became so popular in this country. Isobel is the version found most often in Scotland. Isobella is a latinised form which enjoyed

a vogue during the eighteenth century. Belle and Bella are the usual pet forms.

Isidora, Isadora (f), Isidore (m)
A Greek name which later spread to Spain and was particularly popular with Spanish Jews. Its meaning is obscure, but it possibly derives from 'gift of Isis'. The masculine form is virtually obsolete today, but the feminine version occasionally occurs, possibly because it was the name of the famous American dancer of the 1920s, Isadora Duncan.

Ismay (f)
Sometimes confused with the French-derived Esmé, in fact Ismay is probably of Celtic origin. The meaning is unknown. The name is not found on the Continent and is rare nowadays in Britain.

Isolda, Isolde (f)
This name sounds rather Amazonian in this, the Wagnerian form. The Welsh Essylt has a lighter sound and a prettier meaning. This name is of doubtful origin, with German and Celtic associations. In Old German it means 'ice rule'; in Welsh it is 'fair one'. Isolda was the heroine of the Tristan romances and consequently the name was common in the Middle Ages when the stories were most popular. The French forms Iseut and Isaut were frequently used. The Wagner opera *Tristan und Isolde* stimulated a revival in the German version, which had been obsolete in England for a long time. In Wales, Essylt never went out of use completely.

Ivor (m)
The anglicised spelling of the Welsh name, Ifor, which occurs in Scotland and Ireland as well as Wales. It means 'lord' in Welsh. Ivor was introduced to England from Normandy, where it had developed from the French version Yves.

Ivy (f)
In the nineteenth century there was a vogue for plant and flower names. Ivy was one of them. It's all right, but don't

imagine that because it is short your daughter Ivy will be free of nicknames. Clinging Ivy and Poisoned Ivy are inevitable.

J

Jacinth, Jacintha (f)
The name of a precious stone, which evolved in France from the Greek word for 'hyacinth'. The two Continental versions, Jacinthe and Giacinta, are still used in their respective countries, France and Italy. The English form, Jacinth, appears to have fallen into disuse since the seventeenth century. All three versions are pretty, although the French form would raise pronunciation difficulties. If you like fancy unusual names, either Giacinta or Jacinth is worth consideration.

Jack (m)
Until recent years, anyone named John was very likely to have his proper name forgotten in favour of the pet form Jack. It was so common during the Middle Ages that it became a slang term for man. Jack is still so commonplace that people tend to assume it is the proper name. In fact this is seldom the case.

Jacob (m)
A dignified old Hebrew name from which the classic English name James derived. Jacob has always been a favourite in Jewish families, but although widely used by non-Jews, it generally appeared in an evolved form – Jacopo in Italy, Iago in Spain and Wales, Jacques in France. It is the root of one of those sturdy, uncompromisingly male, single-syllable names which are currently popular in smart circles – Jake. The Hebrew form Jacob came into use in Britain during the seventeenth century, when Bible translators rendered the apostolic name James, in English style, but retained Jacob

for the Old Testament patriarch. The meaning of the name is obscure.

Jacqueline, Jacquetta (f)
Feminine version of the French form of Jacques, which in turn is the equivalent of James in English. Both have been used in Britain without a break ever since their introduction from Belgium during the thirteenth century. Jacqueline is the more popular form today. It is also the version most likely to be shortened to Jackie.

Jake (m)
See Jacob.

James (m)
One of the best of the English versions of biblical names. From the nineteenth century until quite recently, Jim was as universally used for James as Jack was for John. Thankfully, parents appear to have recognised at last that James is too distinguished to be eclipsed permanently behind a nondescript nickname, and are insisting on the proper version at all times. The one short form which is worth using (and sometimes appears as a separate name) is the Scottish Jamie. Seamus is the Irish form, seldom found elsewhere. It is pronounced Shame-us.

Jan (m and f)
The masculine form is a West Country version of John, which has been used from time to time outside that region. For the feminine, see Janet and Janice.

Jane (f)
A consistent favourite, Jane's simplicity gives it a certain beauty, which has never been dispelled although it must be the most popular feminine name in history. Jane has only one drawback. If the girl who bears it is not pretty, she is virtually certain to be teased as 'plain Jane' throughout her childhood. Apart from that, it is perfect. Jane is one of those names which cannot be shortened, so human perversity has evolved pet forms which are longer than the original – Janey and Jenny. Jenny has come to be used as a separate

name. Jane is the relatively modern form of Joanna and Joan, which in turn are the English feminine versions of John. All of them derive from the Old French Jehane, which is pretty enough to be revived. During the eighteenth and nineteenth centuries Jane was popularly linked with other names, producing combinations like Mary Jane and Sarah Jane; but today this treatment sounds outdated. Sheena and Shena are modern renderings of the traditional Irish version of Jane – Sine. In Wales the popular form is Sian (pronounced Shahn).

Janet, Janette (f)
Originally Janet was a diminutive of Jane. Nowadays it is almost always a separate name. Janette is a purely modern variation.

Janice (f)
A diminutive of Jane which has become popular as a separate name in modern times. The short form, Jan, is occasionally used independently.

Jared (m)
Has been used occasionally as a Christian name since the seventeenth century, more often in the USA than in this country. It derives from the Greek words meaning 'rose up'.

Jarvis (m)
See Gervase.

Jasmine (f)
A beautiful flower name which is somehow too fancy to work really well as a forename unless combined with a very simple surname. It is uncommon in Britain today. The name of the jasmine-flower derives from the Persian yasaman.

Jason (m)
Oddly enough, this name, normally associated with Greek legend, is biblical. The best-known Jason was, of course, the hero who sought the Golden Fleece, but use of the name in western countries dates from the seventeenth century, when

it was used as the English rendering of the name of a kins-
man of St Paul. The Greek original was probably Joshua or
Jesus. Jason was one of the names which became too smart
too quickly in the 1960s, and is now unfashionable.

Jasper, Caspar (m)
Old names with a splendidly caddish ring. Choose them only
if you are confident that your son will grow up to be the
sort of dazzling young man who can get away with them.
Casper was the original Eastern version, traditionally the
name of one of the Three Kings. Jaspar, the traditional
English form, apparently evolved during the fourteenth
century. The meaning of the name is unknown.

Jean (f)
Another version of Jane – this time the modern Scottish
form. It is now used throughout Britain. Jennet is the pretty
pet form.

Jeffrey (m)
See Geoffrey.

Jemima (f)
This has a prettily archaic sound today which could make it
ripe for fashionable revival. Jemima comes from the Hebrew
word meaning 'dove', and in the Bible was the name of one
of Job's three daughters. First used in this country during
the seventeenth century, it enjoyed a revival in Victorian
days.

Jennifer (f)
A Cornish form of Guenevere which has survived to become
more popular than the original. Although pretty, it has none
of Guenevere's regal dignity. The short form Jenny is sometimes used as a separate name.

Jeremy (m)
Jeremy is the medieval English form of Jeremiah, the name
of one of the great biblical prophets. Jeremiah has long been
obsolete, but Jeremy has survived to become quite fashion-

able during recent years. The name means 'may Jehovah exalt'. Jerry is the hideous short form.

Jerome (m)
Very occasionally found today, Jerome comes from the ancient Greek words meaning 'sacred name'. St Jerome was deeply revered during the Middle Ages but the name has not been popular since then.

Jerry (m)
The dreadful diminutive of Gerald, Gerard and Jeremy.

Jesse (m)
Beautiful name, which would undoubtedly be in the forefront of the fashionable revival of biblical names, were it not for its sexual ambiguity. When written it is fine; when pronounced it is indistinguishable from the feminine Jessie. Jesse has been used in Britain since the Reformation. It is derived from the Hebrew meaning 'Jehovah exists' and was the name of the father of King David.

Jessica (f)
Used in modern times because of its appearance in Shakespeare's *Merchant of Venice*, Jessica is derived from an old Hebrew name Yiskah, meaning 'God beholds'. Jess is the short form; Jessie is a pet version of Janet, not Jessica.

Jessie (f)
Originally a Scottish diminutive of Janet, it now crops up as a separate name from time to time.

Jethro (m)
Another good, strong biblical name which is likely to be revived. Jethro means 'abundance' in Hebrew. It was used in England after the Reformation.

Jill (f)
This started life as a diminutive of Gillian. It is usually used nowadays as a separate name. A completely neutral name with no distinction; one of those names that are all right if you can think of nothing more interesting.

Joan, Joanna (f)
The oldest English feminine forms of John. These days Joan
sounds rather out-of-date and has been largely replaced by
Jane. Joanna, the latinised version, has retained consider-
ably more distinction and has a somewhat aristocratic image.
A pity that it is so often shortened to Jo.

Jocelyn, Joscelin (m and f)
Uncommon, definitely rather aristocratic, Jocelyn has a lot
going for it. Surprisingly for such a distinguished name, it
combines well with the most commonplace surnames. Even
the short form, Joss, while not really desirable, is not too bad.
The origins of the name are obscure, but it probably derives
from the Latin word meaning 'gay'. The use of Jocelyn as a
girl's name appears to be confined to the present century.

Joel (m)
Biblical name which deserves revival. It means 'Jehovah is
God'. Joel was introduced to England by the Normans. It
has never been common.

John (m)
John Smith used to be cited as the commonest British name,
but we are not alone in our passion for John. It crops up in
Scandinavia and Germany as Jono and Hano, France as Jean,
in the Slavic countries as Jan, in Russia as Ivan, in Italy as
Giovanni and in Spain as Juan. The Celts have separate
versions: Evan, Sion and Ieuan in Wales, Iain in Scotland
and Sean or Shane in Ireland. There is no very clear reason
why it became so popular. It does not appear to have been
used in the West until after the Crusades. The inspiration for
its use appears to have been John the Baptist rather than
John the Evangelist. John is derived from the Hebrew words
meaning 'Grace of the Lord'. The pet form Jack has been
worked to death; the alternative Johnny is less commonplace.

Jolyon (m)
See Julian.

Jonah, Jonas (m)
The biblical Jonah was the worst public relations man this name could have had. It has passed into the English language as a synonym for a bearer of ill luck. As a result it appears to be virtually obsolete today. The medieval English form Jonas appears occasionally in the USA. Jonas means 'dove' in Hebrew.

Jonathan (m)
Not, as may be supposed, a derivation of John, but always a name in its own right. In Hebrew it means 'The Lord has given'. In the Bible, Jonathan was the son of King Saul and friend of David; and the expression David and Jonathan is still used to describe very close friends. Abbreviated, it becomes Jon, not John.

Jordan (m)
Most people associate this with the Palestinian river, but Jordan – it means 'flowing down' in Hebrew – has been used as a forename in Britain since the twelfth century. It is very unusual today, but its splendid individuality makes it merit revival. In the Middle Ages, returning Crusaders were apt to bring home Jordan water to baptise their children, and the name was probably adopted as a result of this custom.

Joscelin (m)
See Jocelyn.

Joseph (m), *Josephine* (f)
Better known in modern times through the short form, Joe, than through the full version. This is a pity; Joseph has a fine sound. Its widespread use in Britain dates from the seventeenth century. It became particularly popular over the years with Roman Catholics, as an expression of growing devotion to the husband of the Virgin Mary. Josephine did not become a proper name until the Empress Josephine of France popularised it. Until then it was a pet form of the French girl's name Marie Josephe.

Joshua (m)
In Hebrew this is the same name as Jesus: they have simply
110

been translated differently. It means 'God is help'. In Latin countries the form Jesus has frequently been used, but Joshua has been the closest approach in the English language. It has been used in Britain since the Reformation, but is rare today. Josh is the unfortunate short form surname.

Joy (f)
Simply the word 'joy' used as a forename. It first appeared in medieval times, died out and was revived during the nineteenth century. It still occurs today and is pleasant enough, if undistinguished.

Joyce (m and f)
Very popular in medieval Britain for both men and women. The spelling then was Josse, a form you may care to revive. By the fourteenth century it had fallen from favour as a man's name, but survived for girls. Joyce suddenly became fashionable during the 1880s and has continued to be widely used, although the vogue for it passed long ago. The meaning of Joyce is obscure, but it is thought to derive from a Breton saint who lived in the seventh century.

Jude (m)
A Biblical name which was never popular because until the Reformation it was used to render in English the name of Judas Iscariot. Since then it has been used as a first name, but only rarely. In Hebrew the original name means 'God will be confessed'.

Judith (f)
Originally simply the Hebrew word meaning 'Jewess', Judith was introduced to England in the ninth century and has been used ever since. The pet form Judy now appears as a separate name. Judith has beauty and dignity. It is also one of those names which is reasonably unusual without being outlandish.

Julia (f)
A graceful feminine form of the Roman clan name Julius. It appears in post-Reformation literature but did not come into everyday use until the eighteenth century. The French

form Julie has enjoyed some popularity in Britain, both as a separate name and as a pet form of Julia, but it lacks the dignity of the latter. Julia has been used in Ireland to anglicise the native Sheila.

Julian (m), Juliana (f)
Derived from the Latin clan name Julius. Both forms are uncommon today, the feminine version marginally less so than the masculine. Both have a definite aristocratic ring but are hard to adapt to the more mundane surnames. John Galsworthy used Jolyon, one of the then-obsolete medieval variations, for a number of his characters in *The Forsyte Saga*. As a result it has been used from time to time as a twentieth century first name.

Juliet (f)
Shakespeare's most romantic heroine bore this name and as a result it has been consistently popular in modern times. Shakespeare probably adapted it from the Italian Giulietta, a pet form of the Italian version of Julia. The French version, Juliette, has been used in this country in modern times.

Julius (m)
A Roman clan name which still survives and flourishes on the Continent as Giulio, Jules and Julio (in Italy, France and Spain respectively) but is virtually obsolete in Britain. Its survival was probably due to the fame of Caius Julius Caesar.

June (f)
Like May and April, June was adopted as a first name for girls born in the appropriate month at the turn of the century. April still has a certain cachet, but May and June sound somewhat dated.

Justin (m), Justine (f)
Once a rare name, except for Byzantine emperors, Justin enjoyed such a vogue in the 1960s that it has become debased. Avoid it if you want a smart or aristocratic name for your son. These days it conjures up an image of scruffy small boys rather than distinguished young men. On the plus

side, it does not lend itself to contractions or nicknames. The feminine form is much more unusual and attractive; but bear in mind that Justin was probably devalued partly because it was used with unsuitable surnames. Justine, a distinguished name, should be used only with an equally distinguished surname. Incidentally it should be pronounced French style, Joosteen, not Just-een. The name is derived from the Latin meaning 'just'.

·K

Karen (f)
A Danish form of Katharine, used as a separate name in Britain during the twentieth century. It was possibly introduced from the USA, where it had been taken by Scandinavian immigrants.

Katharine, Katherine, Catharine, Catherine (f)
A timeless name which has been continuously popular for conturies. Like Helen, it has proved remarkably adaptable, and has all sorts of variations. The original Latin form was Katerina. In Russia this developed into Ekaterina and the diminutives Katya and Katinka. Caterine and Cateline were the French forms. In Middle English the usual versions were Katerine, Katelin or Catlin. The name has always been rich in quite pretty pet forms: Kitty, Katie, Cathy and Kay. Kate, originally a pet form, is currently a fashionable name in its own right. The Irish versions, Cathleen and Kathleen, are now used in England too, as is the Gaelic Catrionas. The origin of the name is obscure, but it is thought to derive from the Greek word meaning 'pure'.

Kathleen (f)
See Katharine.

Katrine (f)
See Katharine.

Kay (m)
One of the knights in the Arthurian legend. The name probably comes from a Welsh translation of the Latin Caius.

Keith (m)
A popular, but not fashionable modern forename adapted from a Scottish surname. It probably derives from the Gaelic word for 'wood' or 'windy place'.

Kenelm (m)
An Old English name that still flourishes – usually as a family tradition. It means 'brave helmet', and was the name of a Mercian saint in the ninth century.

Kenneth (m)
Found in Wales as Cenydd, and in Gaelic regions as Cinead. Kenneth is now used throughout Britain but is essentially a Scottish name. It is derived from the Gaelic word for 'comely'. The unattractive modern short forms are Ken and Kenny.

Kevin (m)
Now found throughout Britain, Kevin originated in Ireland and is still very popular there. In Irish it means 'handsome birth'.

Kim (m and f)
Probably invented by Kipling for the hero of his novel *Kim*. In this case it was an abbreviation of the surname Kimball, used as a forename. In modern times it has figured largely as a girl's name, but in view of the fact that it is also much favoured for dogs, it might be best left alone.

L

Lachlan (m)
Gaelic name still largely confined to the Scottish Highlands.
It derives from the Gaelic meaning 'warlike'.

Laetitia (f)
See Lettice.

Lalage (f)
Unfortunately the modern pronunciation of this Latin name
makes it sound rather soppy. Nowadays it is pronounced
La-layj, whereas the correct classical pronunciation is
La-laggy. In Latin it means 'babble', so perhaps that puts
potential users off it completely. Lalage is very unusual
today.

Lambert (m)
Most often encountered as a surname nowadays, Lambert
became popular as a first name during the twelfth century. It
is derived from the Old German words meaning 'land-
bright'. The most famous bearer of the name was Lambert
Simnel. After his unsuccessful attempt to usurp the English
throne from Henry VII, the name went out of favour. It is
used very occasionally today.

Lancelot (m)
Originally a diminutive of the rather theatrical-sounding
Lance, Lancelot is best known as the name of King Arthur's
most dashing knight. Oddly, Lancelot is not mentioned at all
in the old Welsh sources of the Arthurian legend. He was
introduced in the French version of the tales. Lancelot is
still used sometimes as a forename. It is derived from the
German 'land'.

Laura, Lauretta, Loretta (f)
Like Lawrence, Laura comes from the Latin word meaning

115

'laurel'. It has been used in Britain since the seventeenth century. Lauretta started off as a pet form, but established itself as a separate name. Laura is the prettier version, and, although unusual today, is not so much so as to be outlandish. It is one of the few names around which is hard to shorten, another advantage. Loretta is a modern variation of Lauretta.

Laurence, Lawrence (m)
The Latin term for laurel, from which this name originates, also produced the feminine form Laura. It became common in Britain after the Norman Conquest, and a great many surnames have developed from it. It is still used quite widely, but generally appears in its shortened forms, Larry and Laurie. In fact Laurie, primarily a Scottish development, is distinguished enough to become a separate name.

Lavinia (f)
Sounds old-fashioned, but in the right way. Lavinia does not have the outdated ring which spoils Victorian favourites today, probably because it had been very popular during the eighteenth century and was neglected later as being out of date. Incidentally, it is a favourite gipsy name. If you want an uncommon but traditional name, this could be a good choice. The short form Vinny is occasionally used, but not as a separate name. The meaning is obscure.

Leah (f)
A biblical name which became popular with the Puritans in seventeenth century England. It sounds too much like 'leer' to be popular today – and it means 'cow'!

Lee (f)
See Leonie.

Leila(*h*) (f)
Exotic, attractive name which, although comparatively little-used, has the happy knack of always sounding fashionable. Originally it was the name of the heroine in a popular Persian tale; it means 'dark haired'. Byron used it in a poem with an oriental setting and started a fashion for it.

Lena (f)
A pet form of Helen, now used occasionally as a separate name.

Lenore (f)
See Leonora.

Leo (m)
The Latin word for 'lion'. The name has a somewhat aristocratic ring. Another advantage is that it cannot be shortened; but on the other hand your son will undoubtedly be teased as 'Leo the lion'.

Leonard (m)
Leonard has been used as a forename since the twelfth century, but did not become popular until the Victorian era. It is derived from the Old German 'bold lion'. Today it is fairly common and rather unfashionable. The short forms Len and Lennie are enough to put anyone off using it.

Leonie (f)
French feminine form of Leo. Leona is an alternative version. It is sometimes shortened to Lee.

Leonora, Lenore (f)
These appear to be Continental forms of Eleanor: Leonora is Italian, Lenore German and Leonore French. They became popular during the nineteenth century and are still in use. All are pretty names, but the Italian version is likely to be shortened to Nora.

Leopold (m)
A Continental name little used in England, except for a brief period after Queen Victoria named one of her sons after her Uncle Leopold, King of the Belgians.

Lesley (f), *Leslie* (m)
The masculine version started life as a Scottish surname, derived from a place name. It was not used as a forename before the nineteenth century, when its popularity spread to England. Lesley was coined to provide a feminine version.

Although there is nothing intrinsically wrong with the name, it somehow gives the impression when used for a girl that her parents really wanted a son and have compensated by choosing an adapted masculine name. The ugly short form Les serves both masculine and feminine versions.

Lettice, Laetitia (f)
Lettice is the traditional English form. Laetitia, the Latin version, was introduced during the eighteenth century. In Latin it means 'gladness'. Lettice, with its quaint old-world sound and long tradition, would undoubtedly be ripe for fashionable revival were it not for the name's unfortunate resemblance to a green vegetable. In the 1950s one of the popular girls' comics even carried a strip entitled 'Lettice Leaf, the Greenest Girl in School'. No name survives that sort of punishment!

Lewis, Louis (m)
Lewis was the traditional English style. The lowland Scots adopted the French form, Louis, as in Robert Louis Stevenson. The original name from which both evolved was the Old German Chlodwig. Louis developed from an older French version, Clovis. Clovis deserves revival, if only in memory of the splendidly cynical Clovis Sangrail, invented by Saki and developed through a long series of stories. The traditional Lewis has been used in Wales to anglicise Llewelyn. Ludovic, still used occasionally, is a development of the Latin version, Ludovicus.

Liam (m)
Irish version of William, sometimes used in England since the revival of interest in Celtic names.

Lillian, Lily, Lilla (f)
All originated as pet forms of Elizabeth. The German version, Lili (pronounced Lee-lee) is particularly pretty. By the nineteenth century this form of Lily had lapsed from use, and was revived when flower names became popular.

Lilith (f)
Possibly the most romantic feminine name. Lilith was the

first, archetypal woman. According to Rabbinical literature she was the wife of Adam before Eve was created. Her image was dented somewhat by an early mis-translation of her name as 'night-hag'. In fact it means 'goddess of storms' in Assyro-Babylonian. It takes quite a woman to carry off a name like Lilith, which probably explains its rarity today.

Lina (f)
Pet form of Caroline.

Linda (f)
The derivation of this name – it comes from the Old German for 'snake' – may be a bit off-putting. In fact it should not be. The tribes who used Linda and Lindi as endings of girls' names did so because they held the snake in great reverence for its wisdom and suppleness. Naming a girl after the sacred serpent supposedly conveyed to her a little of these qualities. Linda was not used as a first name in England until the nineteenth century, so its modern derivation here could be from the Spanish word meaning 'pretty'.

Linnet (f)
See Eluned.

Lionel (m)
An old Christian name which probably started life as a derivation of Leo. It has considerable distinction, but suffers from abbreviation to Len or even Li.

Lisette (f)
A French pet form of Elizabeth. It's pretty, but one of those names which are somewhat unfortunate for girls who grow up big and beefy.

Llewelyn (m)
A common Welsh name found less often today than formerly. Its meaning is obscure, but the first syllable appears to stand for 'leader'. There are various spellings, Llewellyn and Llywelyn being the usual variations. Llew is a common short form. In the past Lewis has been used as an anglicisation.

Lloyd (m)
A common Welsh surname and forename. It has not been widely adopted in England but occurs quite frequently in America. Llwyd was the original Welsh spelling. It means 'grey'.

Lois (f)
A biblical name with an oddly modern sound. It was adopted by the Puritans in the seventeenth century. Lois is of Greek origin, but its meaning is unknown. It should be pronounced as a two-syllable name – Low-iss, not as Loyss.

Lola (f)
A diminutive of the Spanish Dolores, very occasionally used in Britain as an independent name. Lola seems to have acquired a similar exotic image to that of another diminutive which crops up as an independent name – Sadie.

Lolita (f)
See Lola.

Loretta (f)
A corruption of Loreto, a famous Italian pilgrimage town. The use of Loretta is virtually confined to Roman Catholic families.

Lorna (f)
First saw the light of day as the heroine of R. D. Blackmore's novel *Lorna Doon*. Blackmore is believed to have adapted the name from the title of the Marquesses of Lorne. It is fairly uncommon today.

Lorraine (f)
A modern French forename adapted from the German place-name Lotharingen. This century it has spread to Britain and North America.

Lottie (f)
See Charlotte.

Louis (m)
See Lewis.

Louisa, Louise (f)
Adaptations of the French masculine Louis. Louise was the original version, first used in England during the seventeenth century. Louisa, the native British form, developed in the eighteenth century. The pet form is Louie. Both names are enjoying a fashionable revival at present.

Loveday (f)
A delightful medieval forename which has virtually died out everywhere except in Cornwall, and deserves a revival. Originally a loveday was a day appointed for settlement meetings between enemies or opposing parties in a lawsuit. It was given as a name to boys and girls born on such days, but was later confined to girls.

Lucia, Lucy (f)
A feminine form of the Roman name derived from the word lux – 'light'. In ancient times, Lucia was often chosen for children born at dawn. Lucy and Luce were the English versions of the name. Other variations are Lucette, Lucinda, Lucasta and Lucilla. Lucy is by far the most popular version today.

Lucian (m)
A rare modern form of the Roman name Lucianus, used from time to time in Britain since the nineteenth century. Originally a Greek word, its meaning is obscure.

Lucilla, Lucinda (f)
See Lucia.

Lucretia (f)
One would have thought that the notorious Lucrezia Borgia's evil reputation would have prevented anyone from choosing the name in later years, but apparently it was quite popular in Lancashire until the late eighteenth century. It is virtually obsolete today. Lucretia is derived from a Roman clan name.

121

Ludovic (m)
See Lewis.

Luke (m)
Terribly trendy – you won't find it in *The Times*' top names
list yet, but it has arrived, just as Emma, Dominic, Jake
and Benedict once did. In fact it's a very beautiful old name,
occasionally also found in Britain in its Latin form, Lucas.
St Luke the Evangelist was patron saint of physicians and
of painters; and craftsmen frequently gave the name to their
sons in past generations.

Lydia (f)
Enjoyed a brief vogue in Britain during the seventeenth
century, but has never been common. It is derived from the
Greek for 'girl from Lydia', and was the name of a widow
who, according to the Acts of the Apostles, was converted
by St Paul when he stayed at her house.

Lynn(e) (f)
A modern name derived from the Old English word meaning
'pool' or 'waterfall'. It's very widely used today, but has little
distinction.

M

Mabel, Mabella (f)
A drearily pedestrian traditional English form of Amabel.
Mably, Mabbit and Mabbot were early variations that are
now obsolete. After a long decline, Mabel suddenly surged
back into fashion in the late nineteenth century. The vogue
has disappeared now and it is a very outdated name.

Madeleine, Madeline, Magdalen (f)
Magdalen, the beautiful original form of this name, suffered
two disadvantages in Britain: magdalen was a polite term for

a prostitute; and in English it was pronounced Maudlin – a word that developed to mean weak and sentimental. The name derives from the Hebrew 'woman of Magdala' – the birthplace of Mary Magdalene. The French version, Madeleine, has been used in this country since the twelfth century. Maddy and Magda have been used as short forms in modern times.

Madge (f)
See Margaret.

Madoc (m)
An Old Welsh forename which developed into the surname Maddox and Maddocks. It means 'fortunate'. Still used in Wales, although not common even there, it is virtually never found in England.

Magda, Magdalen (f)
See Madeleine.

Magnus (m)
Just the name you need to give your son a splendidly Viking image. In fact it is derived from Latin, and means 'great'. It was allegedly adopted as a forename by accident, when the Latin rendering of Charlemagne's combined name and title – Carolus Magnus – was thought to be a name. It has been the name of many Danish and Norwegian kings and is occasionally used in Britain.

Maisie (f)
A Scottish diminutive of Margaret, which enjoyed a brief spell of popularity as an independent name during the 1930s.

Malcolm (m)
A favourite Scottish forename which is now widely used in England too. It is derived from the Gaelic meaning 'follower of St Columba'.

Malvina (f)
Anglicised rendering of Gaelic Macl-mhin – 'smooth brow', seldom found today.

123

Manuel (m)
See Emmanuel.

Mahra (f)
A pretty and unusual name, which, unfortunately, means 'bitter' in Hebrew.

Marcella, Marcelle (f)
Marcella is virtually obsolete now and the French version, Marcelle, is not popular. Originally Marcella was the name of a Roman widow who was a disciple of St Jerome.

Marcia (f)
Occasionally used as a feminine form for Marcus. Marcie is the pet form.

Marcus, Mark (m)
Mark is currently suffering from over-exposure. It was too popular at the same time as Adam in the 1960s. Marcus, on the other hand, is very up and coming. The name is a Roman derivation from Mars, the god of war. Both versions have the marvellous advantage of being hard to abbreviate or modify.

Margaret (f)
The Greeks adapted this name from the Persian original, and it has been used widely in many countries ever since. It means 'pearl'. The French forms, Marguerite and Margot, have occasionally been popular in Britain and are still used. Margery or Marjorie, an early variation, swiftly established itself as an independent name. Pet forms include Meg, Peg, Maggie, Maisie, Greta (from the German form) and Rita (from the Italian). Rita and Greta now exist as independent names, too. Madge is a commonplace modern short form.

Margery, Marjorie (f)
Developed from the French form of Margaret, Marguerite. Marjorie was the Scottish spelling, Margery the English. In the USA Margery is frequently shortened to Margy.

Maria (f)
See Mary.

Mariabella (f)
A compound name invented when such combinations were fashionable early in the seventeenth century. Christabel and Claribel are other examples. It is still used, but rarely.

Marie (f)
See Mary.

Mariel (f)
A German pet form of Mary, now used occasionally in Britain as an independent name.

Marietta (f)
Adapted as a girl's name from the town of Marietta, Ohio, in the USA. Nowadays occasionally encountered in Britain.

Marigold (f)
One of the flower names adopted for girls in the Edwardian era. Not popular today.

Marilyn (f)
A fancy modern derivation of Mary, immortalised by the film star, Marilyn Monroe. No one else could possibly get away with it.

Marina (f)
Became popular in Britain after the wedding of the Greek Princess Marina to Prince George, later Duke of Kent, in 1934. It is derived from the Latin adjective meaning 'of the sea'. Marina and Mairenni are also gipsy names.

Marion, Marian(ne) (f)
Marion was originally a French diminutive of Mary, which became popular as a separate name. When double names came into fashion in the eighteenth century, Marion and Marianne appeared as combinations of Anne and Mary.

Marius (m)
Never achieved the popularity in Britain which the variation, Mario, enjoyed in Italy. It is still used, but rarely. Marius developed from the Roman family name.

Mark (m)
See Marcus.

Marmaduke (m)
One of those names which, for some unknown reason, make people giggle. That is an excellent reason for not bestowing it upon your son. It is derived from the Irish for 'servant of Madoc'.

Martha (f)
In the Bible story, Mary Magdalene had the glamorous image and her sister Martha was the plain home-maker. Martha means 'lady' in Aramaic. It did not appear in Britain until after the Reformation. Martita and Martella are modern derivations of the name, which is now rather out of fashion. Marty is a pet form.

Martin (m), *Martina* (f)
From the Latin meaning 'of Mars'. St Martin was a favourite saint in England and France, so his name became very popular. The masculine form is still in regular use, but the feminine version, never popular, has become virtually obsolete.

Mary (f)
Like Jane, always one of the most popular English names. It has the advantage of being simple, traditional and difficult to debase (we will ignore those unspeakable people who shorten it to Mare). Its one drawback is its popularity. No one approaches a Mary and says 'What a beautiful name!' although nobody says it's ugly, either. If you like the tradition but want something less commonplace, choose a variation. The original Hebrew form was Miriam, later translated in the Bible as Mariam or Maria. The French version, Marie, is widely used in Britain. Among diminutives Marion and Mariot have been popular in the past. Be wary of pet forms. Molly and Polly are quite pretty, but Minnie, Mamie and May sound dated today.

Matilda, Maud(e) (f)
Favourite medieval name, derived from the Old German

'battle strength'. Effectively they are the same name, Matilda the Latin version, Maud the French. Both were used in England. Early variations included Matillis and Mould. Till and Tillot were the popular nicknames. It fell into disuse for centuries, but Matilda became popular once more in the 1700s and Maud enjoyed a revival during the nineteenth century thanks to Tennyson's poem of that name. Matilda is quite fashionable today, but Maud is definitely not. The modern pet form Tildy is quite pretty. Tilly is less so.

Matthew, Matthias (m)
Considered old-fashioned for some time, Matthew is making a very strong come-back – but NOT attended by the awful short forms Matt and Matty. It is in vogue with the same people who call their sons Luke, Benjamin and Daniel. Matthew derives from the Hebrew 'gift of Jehovah'. Macy was an early pet form. Matthias, the Latin version, is little used today.

Maud(e) (f)
See Matilda.

Maura (f)
See Moira.

Maureen (f)
An Irish equivalent of Mary which spread throughout Britain as a separate name as a result of its popularity in the USA. In Irish it is Mairin, a diminutive of Maire. The modern short forms, Mo and Reeny, are hideous.

Maurice, Morris (m)
Maurice developed from the French version, Meurice, but Morris was the native British form. It comes from the Latin term for 'Moor'. Maurice is the usual modern spelling. It is not a fashionable name at present, although still widely used. Meurig, the Welsh version, still occurs (it is pronounced My-rig).

Mavis (f)
Until the turn of the century, this was simply an old word

127

for thrush. Then Marie Corelli used it in a novel and it enjoyed some popularity as a girl's name. Not uncommon today, it has little distinction.

Maximilian (m)
A favourite name in Germany, where it was devised by the Emperor Frederick III as a combination of the names of two great Roman generals. These days it seldom appears in Britain, and usually then in the short version, Max.

Maxine (f)
Maxine, like Roxy, is a name they used to give to cinemas. Would you call your daughter Roxy? If not, think twice about Maxine, too.

May (f)
See Mary. Also used as a separate name associated with the month, like April and June.

Meave (f)
Name of a legendary Irish queen, sometimes rendered in English as Mab.

Melanie, Melloney (f)
Melanie was to fashionable parents in the 1950s what Samantha became in the 1960s and Emma seems set to be for the 1970s. As a result it is currently rather out of style, but it is pretty and will undoubtedly be revived. Melanie means 'black' in Greek. It was introduced to Britain from France by Huguenot refugees, and has always been particularly popular in Devon and Cornwall.

Melior(a) (f)
A rare name, apparently exclusively used in Cornwall. It was largely replaced by Amelia.

Melissa (f)
A pretty name which enjoyed a brief vogue during the eighteenth century and is now becoming fashionable once more. In Greek it means 'a bee', but was also the name of a nymph. Italian poets intensified Melissa's graceful image in

128

the sixteenth century by using it as the name of a fairy. Watch out for the awful pet form Melly.

Melloney (f)
See Melanie.

Melody (f)
A simple adoption of a noun as a first name, but as fancy names go, this has quite an old tradition. It was in use in Shropshire as early as the eighteenth century.

Meraud (f)
One of a number of old English names that appear to occur only in Cornwall. Its origin is obscure, but possibly it comes from the Cornish word for 'sea'. Very rare today, even in Cornwall.

Mercedes (f)
No, the car was named after the girl, not the girl after the car! Her name was Mercedes Jellinek, and you must admit that Mercedes-Benz sounds far more romantic than Jellinek-Benz. Mercedes was originally a 'substitute' name for Mary, in countries where Mary was considered too sacred for everyday use. In this case the substitution derived from Maria de Mercedes – Spanish for *'Mary of Mercies'*. Mercedes is popular in Spain, France, and, to a lesser extent, Germany. It is occasionally found in Britain. It is a beautiful name, but does not adapt readily to many British surnames.

Mercy (f)
One of the virtue names which became popular with the Puritans in seventeenth century England. It is still used. Other examples are Faith, Hope, Charity and Verity.

Meredith (m and f)
The anglicised version of the Welsh Maredudd, now a common surname in Wales and still found as a first name for men. In the USA it has appeared from time to time as a girl's name, too, and as such has been re-introduced to England. As a feminine name it is extremely unusual here.

The meaning is obscure, but suggested interpretations are 'great chief' or 'lord from the sea'.

Meriel (f)
See Muriel.

Merle (f)
In use as a first name in Britain since the nineteenth century, Merle has never been common. It is the French word for 'blackbird'. Has the advantage of simplicity, but works with few English surnames.

Merlin, Merlyn (m)
From the Welsh Myrddin, 'sea hill'. It is still used, but rarely. Indelibly associated with the great magician of the Arthurian legend. Mervyn, more popular in England, is a modern derivation.

Mervyn (m)
See Merlin.

Michael (m), *Michaela* (f)
Very popular throughout Britain today, this name is particularly common in Ireland, where it is generally abbreviated to Mick. Michael was one of the seven biblical archangels. The name means 'who is like the Lord?' in Hebrew. As the leader of the Heavenly Host, Michael became the patron saint of Christian warriors. Early versions were spelled differently from the modern form, occurring as Mighel, Mihel and Miel. Miles, at first a pet form, later became a separate name which has endured until the present. The feminine form Michaela is modern. In France, the feminine versions Michele and Michelle have been established longer, and have enjoyed a rash of popularity in Britain since the War. Apart from Mick, common abbreviations for the masculine form include Mike, Micky and Mitch.

Mildred (f)
Like many old names which enjoyed a burst of popularity in the nineteenth century, Mildred now sounds terribly outdated, and is no longer popular. It is derived from the Old

English words meaning 'merciful strength'. It is still used as a gipsy name. Mildred shares with Millicent the pet form, Milly.

Miles (m)
Derived from one of two sources – either from an early pet form of Michael, or from the Old German Milo. The Normans introduced Miles to England. It has become increasingly popular during the twentieth century. In Ireland the form Milo still survives, possibly because the name was used originally to render the Irish Maolmuire, 'servant of Mary'.

Millicent, Melicent, Melisande (f)
Introduced to England from France in the twelfth century, this name was originally spelled Melisent. It derives from an Old German name which combines the words 'work' and 'strong'. Malasintha was an early variation. It is unusual today but sounds prettily traditional enough to qualify as a 'smart' name. Milly and Melly are the usual pet forms.

Mina (f)
A pet form of Wilhelmina, occasionally used as a separate name.

Minna (f)
An Old German name derived from the word for 'love', which was used in Shetland and other parts of Scotland before spreading to England when Scott used it in a novel. Very uncommon today.

Mirabel, Mirabelle (f)
From the Latin meaning 'glorious' or 'wonderful', this pretty name has been debased by its use as the title of a romantic strip cartoon magazine launched in the 1950s. The spelling Mirabelle is modern; Mirabel is the original version, used in Britain since the twelfth century. Mirable and Marabel were early variations.

Miranda (f)
Pleasing name with an indefinable aristocratic quality. In

Latin it means 'worthy to be admired'. Miranda was apparently coined as a girl's name by Shakespeare, for his heroine in *The Tempest*. Like other Shakespearean names (Imogen, Hero, Juliet) it has been quite popular throughout the twentieth century.

Miriam (f)
The beautiful Hebrew original of Mary, meaning 'desired child'. Always a favourite in Jewish families, it became popular with Christians after the Reformation. See also Mary.

Moira, Moyra (f)
An anglicised version of the Irish form of Mary – Maire. Quite widely used in England, but not very fashionable.

Molly (m)
Originally a pet form of Mary; now frequently used as a separate name.

Mona (f)
Adopted in England when Irish names became fashionable in the nineteenth century. It is derived from the Irish word meaning 'noble'. It has a somewhat dated image today, although it is still used.

Monday (f)
In the Middle Ages, this was used for daughters who were born on Monday. Friday and Saturday were similarly used, but the other days were, for some reason, ignored. In modern times, Tuesday has enjoyed some popularity because of the film starlet Tuesday Weld, but the other 'day' names appear to be obsolete.

Monica (f)
A name of unknown origin and meaning, Monica has long been used in France as Monique. It first appeared in England early in the seventeenth century. Widely used today, but not fashionable.

Montagu(e) (m)
This started life as a Norman surname, derived from Mont
Aigu near Caen in northern France. Like other aristocratic
surnames, it has appeared as a first name in relatively
modern times.

Morag (f)
A Scottish name now sometimes used in England. It is
derived from the Gaelic for 'great', and in Scotland is sometimes used instead of Sarah.

Morgan (m and f)
The two earliest forms of this Celtic name meant 'sea-
bright' and 'seaborn'. Morgan is still a popular masculine
forename in Wales, and a very common surname. For girls,
it is less widely used, but the tradition is an ancient one.
Queen Morgan-le-Fay, the great Celtic enchantress, Queen
of Air and Darkness in the Arthurian legend, bore it. Morgan
is a lovely name for either sex, and not easily shortened or
corrupted. Even the Welsh, who manage some sort of nickname for most things, can only come up with the dreadful
Mog – and that is mercifully rare.

Morwen, Morwenna (f)
A Welsh name weaning 'sea wave' or 'sea form'. Seldom
found outside Wales.

Moses (m)
Like Abraham, there is something too patriarchal about
Moses for it to be popular in modern Britain. Its meaning is
uncertain, possibly Egyptian rather than Hebrew.

Moyra (f)
See Moira.

Mungo (m)
A Gaelic name still largely confined to Scotland. It means
'beloved'.

Murdoch (m)
Nowadays more commonplace as a surname, but still found

as a first name, Murdoch is from the Gaelic 'sea-man'. It is popular in Scotland and is found occasionally south of the border. The Irish version is Murtagh.

Muriel, Meriel, Meryl (f)
Possibly derived from the Irish version of the Celtic 'sea-bright', this name was introduced to England from Normandy in the thirteenth century. Muriel, Meriel and Miriel were all common at that period. Maryell was a later variation. It gradually dropped out of use, was reported as almost obsolete by the mid-nineteenth century, but by the 1880s was enjoying a fashionable revival, as both Muriel and Meriel. Since then Muriel has gone out of style once more, possibly because of over-use. Meriel still occurs, as do the modern developments, Merrill and Meryl. Mireille is the French version.

Murray (m)
Originally a Scottish surname, Moray, it developed as a first name in deference to the famous James Stuart, Earl of Moray and half-brother to Mary Queen of Scots. The name gradually evolved as Murray. It is more widely used in Scotland than in England.

Myfanwy (f)
Probably the best of the Welsh Christian names, Myfanwy has been used only rarely in England because it looks hard to pronounce. In fact it is quite simple – M'vanwee. It is a pity that in Wales so many people shorten it to Van and Vano. The name means 'my rare one'.

Myra (f)
Invented in the sixteenth century for poetic use by Lord Brooke, Myra continued to be found purely in literature until the nineteenth century. It is not fashionable nowadays, but still occurs quite frequently.

Myrtle (f)
A nineteenth century invention, adopted from the shrub of that name. Very dated.

134

N

Nadine (f)
An attractive, somewhat exotic name introduced to England during the twentieth century. The original form is the Russian Nadezhda – 'hope'. Nadine is the French version. The diminutives Nadia and Nada are also found.

Nan, Nancy (f)
See Ann.

Naomi (f)
A biblical name which so far has not joined the popular revival. It means 'pleasance', and was the name of Ruth's mother-in-law. Naomi has been used as a forename in Britain since the seventeenth century.

Natalie, Natalia, Natasha (f)
An ideal choice for the daughter born on Christmas day – it means 'birthday of the Lord'. Natalie and its variations are much prettier than the other 'Christmas' girl's name, Noelle. The diminutive, Natasha, is a favourite in Russia.

Nathan (m)
Jewish families have, sensibly, been using this sturdy, attractive name for years, but it has never been popular among gentiles. It comes from the Hebrew for 'gift', and was the name of the Old Testament prophet who condemned King David for sending Uriah to the front line of battle so that David would have a chance of marrying his beautiful wife, Bathsheba. The diminutive, Nat, is without charm.

Nathanael, Nathaniel (m)
This has a similar derivation to Nathan. Nathaniel means 'God has given'. It was not used widely in England until after the Reformation. Then it became quite commonplace. It is usually shortened to Nat.

Neil (m)
See Nigel.

Nell (f)
See Helen.

Nessie, Nest, Nesta (f)
Welsh forms of Agnes.

Netta, Nettie (f)
Scottish diminutives of Janet.

Neville (m)
One of the great aristocratic houses of the Middle Ages, the Nevilles came to England with the Conqueror and derived their surnames from Neuville in Normandy. It has been used as a first name since the early seventeenth century, and is still current, though not commonplace. Nev is the somewhat undignified short form.

Niall (m)
See Nigel.

Nicholas (m), *Nicola, Nicolette* (f)
The traditional English form of this name is little used today but is most attractive – Nicol. It was extremely popular in the Middle Ages but fell from grace around the Reformation period. Nicholas is derived from the Greek word meaning 'victory'. St Nicholas is the patron saint of children, sailors, pawnbrokers and, oddly, wolves. Originally the name was spelled Nicolas, as the feminine form still is. Nick, Nicky and Nichol are the modern short forms. Colin, formerly another popular abbreviation, is now a name in its own right. Nicholas was so popular that it evolved into a huge variety of surnames, including Nixon, Collins, Colet and Cole. Nicola and Nicolette are, respectively, the Italian and French feminine forms. The English version, now extinct, was Nicolaa. Colette and Nicole are fairly commonplace in France and appear occasionally in Britain.

Nigel, Niall, Neil (m)
A much-travelled name which spread from Ireland, where it
originated, to Iceland, thence to Scandinavia and Norman
France. From Normandy it was introduced to England. The
original Irish form was Niul, derived from the word for
'champion'. In Iceland it was Njal, in Normandy Nel or Nele.
Nigellus was the Latinisation from which Nigel evolved.
Niall, now the accepted Irish form, is the most accurate spelling. Neal is probably the most modern version, which has
been re-adopted as a first name after developing as a surname.

Nina (f)
A Russian diminutive of Anne, used occasionally in Britain
as a separate forename. The French versions, Ninon and
Ninette, are much rarer here.

Ninian (m)
Now found largely in Scotland, Ninian was the name of an
early Christian saint. The meaning of the name is obscure.

Nita (f)
Nita now appears occasionally as a name in its own right,
particularly in the USA. In fact it is a diminutive of the
Spanish Juanita, itself a pet form of Juana (Joan). Anita is
a similarly-formed diminutive of Anne.

Noel (m), *Noelle* (f)
An alternative to Christmas or Natalie for children born on
Christmas Day, this name has been in use for such a purpose
since the Middle Ages. Today it is sometimes used when
there is no connection with the religious festival, simply
because parents like the name. Neither form is particularly
common.

Nona (f)
This should be given only to a ninth child, as it means 'ninth'
in Latin and, like Decimus, came into use when families were
large in the nineteenth century. However this and the derivation Anona achieved some popularity earlier this century
and were applied whether or not the child was the ninth.

137

Nonie (f)
Pet form of Nora, sometimes used as a separate name.

Nora (*h*) (f)
Irish abbreviation of Honora, which has been an independent
name for many years.

Noreen (f)
Irish variation of Nora.

Norma (f)
Bellini's opera, *Norma*, made this name popular in the nineteenth century. It has been used widely since then, but is not
particularly popular or fashionable today. It is probably
derived from the Latin word meaning 'rule'.

Norman (m)
A corruption of the Old English and German words for
'northman', used extensively in England as a forename since
before the Conquest. It spread to Scotland, surviving there
after the name died out in England during the fourteenth
century. Re-introduced from Scotland in the nineteenth
century, Norman enjoyed some popularity. It is still used
today, but is unfashionable. The modern diminutive Norm
must be one of the worst ever devised.

Norris (m)
A name originally used by the French to describe Vikings, it
means 'northerner'. Although uncommon today, Norris is
still used.

O

Oberon (m)
See Aubrey.

Obedience (f)
Another of those virtue names so popular with the seven-teenth century Puritans. Unlike many others, Obedience is not a likely candidate for revival. It's hardly a quality which goes with liberated womanhood!

Octavia (f), *Octavius* (m)
Another 'number' name which became rare as big families fell from favour. This one means 'eighth' in Latin. It was also a Roman clan name, and the feminine form seems to have survived, possibly as a development from this source rather than the eighth child. Tavie was a popular Edwardian pet form for the feminine version.

Odette (f)
See Ottilia.

Ogier (m)
Now obsolete in England, but still used in Scandinavia. Ogier le Danois (Holger the Dane) was one of the great heroes in the Charlemagne romance. In Denmark there is a story that he sleeps beneath the foundations of Kronborg Castle, and will wake to save his country if it is in danger. A splendid statue of Holger can be seen in the castle dungeons.

Olaf (m)
See Oliver.

Olga (f)
A favourite Russian name which evolved from the Norse Helga – 'holy'. Along with other Russian names like Vera and Sonia, it was introduced to Britain in the nineteenth century. Olga has been used regularly since then, but never achieved much popularity.

Olive, Olivia(f), *Oliver* (m)
Masculine and feminine forms of this name are both derived from foreign words meaning 'olive' – Olivia from the Latin, Oliver from the French Olivier. Olive has gone out of fashion over the past generation, but Olivia is quite popular. Traditional English forms included Oliff and the diminutives

Olivet and Ollett. Oliver was a favourite masculine name in medieval times because the most famous of Charlemagne's legendary paladins had borne it. As most of the names in the Charlemagne romances are of Teutonic origin, it is likely that Oliver derived from the Norse Olaf, or even the Old German Alfihar – 'elf-host'. Reaction against Oliver Cromwell drove the name out of fashion after the Restoration in England, and it was not revived until the end of the nineteenth century. The old short form Noll has disappeared today, and the modern abbreviation Ollie is current. The French version, Olivier, is very occasionally found.

Olwen (f)
The original Olwen was a legendary Welsh princess, whose lover enlisted the aid of King Arthur to win her in marriage. The name means 'white footprints' and she was called Olwen because it was said that white flowers sprung up wherever she trod. It was a popular name in Wales for many years, and spread to England in the 1840s when a new translation of the Welsh book of legends, *The Mabinogion*, was published.

Oonagh (f)
See Una.

Ophelia (f)
This has acquired a somewhat unfortunate image thanks to the rather spineless Ophelia who went mad in Shakespeare's *Hamlet*. It is derived from the Greek word meaning 'help', but does not seem to have been used before the sixteenth century. It still appears occasionally in Britain and the USA.

Oriana (f)
A name used by sixteenth century poets for Queen Elizabeth I. It is thought to derive from the Latin word for 'dawn'. It has always been very rare apart from this use, but still occurs from time to time. It would be very difficult to match to a surname.

Oriel (f)
A delightful and rare name compounded from the Old

German words for 'fire' and 'strife'. Well worth a modern revival.

Orlando (m)
There was a fashion for Italian names in sixteenth century England, when this, the Italian form of Roland, came into vogue. It is still used and has the right distinguished air to become a fashionable favourite. But do remember that it was also the name of the marmalade cat in the stories, and that your little Orlando may suffer some ribbing as a result.

Osbert (m)
An ancient name which was quite popular at the end of the nineteenth century, although it has now declined again. It means 'bright god' in Old English.

Oscar (m)
This suffered a crippling blow when Oscar Wilde was jailed for homosexuality. When it started to recover, someone used it as a nickname for the American Academy Award presented in the film industry. That appears to have been the *coup de grace* as far as Britain was concerned, but it is still used in the USA. It means 'godspear' in Old English.

Osmond (m)
Nowadays Osmond is more familiar as a surname, but it still appears now and then as a first name. It means 'God's protection' in Old English.

Oswald (m)
An Old English name, now unfashionable, although it still occurs. It means 'God's power'.

Ottilia, Ottilie (f)
Ottilia is the original form which we derive from Old German, but on the rare occasions when the name appears today, it is generally in the modern form of Ottilie. Odille is the French version, with the diminutive Odette. Both have been used at times in Britain. The name is derived from the Old German word for 'fatherland'.

Owain, Owen (m)
Traditionally one of the most popular Welsh names. Still
widely used in Wales. Its origins are obscure: it could derive
from the Welsh word for 'lamb' or from Ewen, meaning
'youth'. Owen is now used throughout Britain and the USA.

P

Paddy (m and f)
See Patricia, Patrick.

Pagan (m)
Strictly for the self-confident, avent-garde parent. Originally
it did not mean 'heathen', but 'peasant' or 'rustic'. Introduced to England by the Normans, it was the basis of surnames like Payne. The name was used regularly until the
Reformation, then went out of favour, never to be revived.
It is so off-beat and glamorous that it could well make a
come-back.

Pamela (f)
Sir Philip Sydney coined Pamela as a woman's name for
his romance *Arcadia* in 1590. It remained a literary name
until Samuel Richardson used it for the heroine of a novel
of the same name in the eighteenth century. Since then it has
been very widely used. Today we pronounce it differently
from the original version, which was pronounced Pameela.
It is a rather nondescript name, with an unattractive short
form, Pam. Pamela derives from the Greek words meaning
'all honey'.

Pat, Patty (f)
See Patricia.

Patience (f)
Adopted as a first name in seventeenth century England by

the Puritans, along with other 'virtues' like Charity and Verity. Some Puritans appear to have developed mild obsessions about such names; Sir Thomas Carew, Speaker of the House of Commons in early Stuart days, had daughters named Patience, Temperance, Silence and Prudence. Some of these names are charming and, deservedly, are still used. Silence and Obedience have been dropped, probably because women are regarded in a somewhat different light today.

Patricia (f)
Although derived from Roman origins, Patricia was not adopted as a forename in Britain until the eighteenth century. It became really popular when one of Queen Victoria's granddaughters was christened Patricia. Pat, Paddy, Patty and Trisha are found as modern short forms, some of them appearing as independent names. Like Shirley and Jill, Pat was very popular during the 1930s. The name originally did no more than denote a female member of the Roman Patrician class.

Patrick (m)
The archetypal Irish name. This, the Latin for 'nobleman', was adopted at his ordination by St Patrick. It is so much an Irish name that the short form, Paddy, is a universal nickname for Irishmen, just as Jock signifies a Scot and Taffy a Welshman. Patrick was originally far more popular in Ireland and Scotland than in England, but today its use is spread throughout Britain. It remains the most commonplace man's name in Ireland. There Pat and Patsy, as well as Paddy, are used as short forms.

Paul (m)
For some reason Paul was always less popular than the other major biblical names. During the seventeenth century it enjoyed a measure of popularity, but this was largely because Peter, the papal name, was out of favour in Protestant England. Nowadays it is fairly popular. The name means 'small' in Latin. In the New Testament, Saul of Tarsus adopted the name after his conversion to Christianity on the Road to Damascus. As a modern choice, it has various advantages: no nicknames (except perhaps the rather coy

143

Paulie); a long tradition and a happy ability to combine well with just about any modern surname.

Paula, Paulina, Pauline (f)
Relatively modern feminine forms of Paul, the former from the German version, the others from the Latin. Pauline is the best known, and in France is the universal feminine form of Paul. Paula is gradually becoming more fashionable in England. The pet form Polly is occasionally found.

Pearl (f)
This is now very dated. Pearl became fashionable during the nineteenth century along with other gem names like Ruby and Beryl. Before it was used in this context, it often occurred as a pet form of Margaret (derived from the Greek word meaning 'pearl').

Peggy (f)
See Margaret.

Penelope (f)
Although Penelope appears in the Homeric epics, the name was not adopted for everyday use in England until the sixteenth century. Penelope was the faithful wife of Odysseus. The name has retained its somewhat aristocratic tone because it has never been over-used. In Ireland it has been used to anglicise the native name Fionnghuala. There is a pretty gipsy name which may have derived from Penelope – Peneli. Usual short form is Penny.

Penny (f)
See Penelope.

Pentecost (m and f)
It was an old custom to name children born on Christian feast days after the particular feast. Easter and Christmas are still found occasionally, but Pentecost, once just as popular, has probably now become obsolete.

Perceval, Percival (m)
A romantic name invented in the Middle Ages for the hero

of a poem by the French troubador Chrétien de Troyes. It gradually spread to England, but has never been popular.

Percy (m)
Surprisingly, not a short form of Percival but a separately-derived name. Percy started off as a forename inside the Percy family when they adapted their own surname for the purpose. Over the years it spread outside the family and during the nineteenth century its use became general. It is not fashionable or widely used today.

Perdita (f)
An exquisite, off-beat name invented by Shakespeare for the heroine of *A Winter's Tale*. It is the Latin word meaning 'lost'. Take care about combining it with a suitable surname, and don't let anyone shorten it to Perdy.

Peregrine (m)
This is so aristocratic that with the wrong surname it can sound like a send-up of itself, so be careful. The name means 'stranger' or 'traveller' in Latin, and is also the name of a species of falcon. It is unusual. Perry is the short form, for once not a bad one, either.

Perpetua (f)
Generally used only by Roman Catholic families. Perpetua was a virgin martyr of Carthage, who was later canonised. The name means 'perpetual' in Latin.

Peter (m)
Everyone must know that Peter means 'rock'. The biblical interpretation of St Peter as the rock on which Christ would base his church has apparently affected the name's image, for it invariably conjures up a picture of steadiness and reliability. Classless, it sits as well on a dustman as on a duke. Pete is an undesirable abbreviation, but otherwise the name has few pitfalls. Not for those who are looking for something unusual. If you like the name but find it too humdrum, go back to the original English form, derived from Old French – Piers. Peter was unknown until the fourteenth century.

Petra (f)
See Petronella.

Petronella, Petronilla (f)
Feminine forms of Peter. The Latin noun meaning 'stone',
Petra has also been used as a feminine name in modern
times, and nowadays probably occurs more often than
Petronella. One very pretty medieval contraction of the
name is worth reviving for independent use. It is Peronel.

Petula (f)
A modern feminine name derived from the Latin word
meaning 'seeker'. It has little distinction and suffers the
appalling short form Pet.

Philip (m), *Philippa* (f)
The legion of British surnames derived from Philip testify
to its popularity in the Middle Ages. It was very popular
until the reign of Mary Tudor, when the queen made an
unpopular marriage with King Philip of Spain. The name
never recovered from this blow to its prestige and was rare
until its revival during the nineteenth century. Although
widely used, it is not commonplace, and has a quiet distinction about it in spite of the unattractive and sexually
ambiguous short form Phil. The feminine form was not used
until the nineteenth century, except as a written distinction
between Philip as a male and as a female name. During the
Victorian era the pretty Italian abbreviation Pippa was
adopted, both as a pet form and as a separate name.

Phoebe (f)
A pretty Greek name meaning 'shining one', which can be
difficult for everyday use because a lot of people hesitate
over the pronunciation. It has two syllables, not one as is so
often supposed. Pronounce it Feebee, not Fobe.

Phyllis, Phillida (f)
A name much used by Greek and Roman pastoral poets. The
original Phyllis hanged herself for love and was turned into a
tree. If you think your daughter can cope with that, it's a
pretty name. Phillida was an English version coined in the
146

eighteenth century. If you want something unusual, it is much rarer today than Phyllis. Like Philip, these two names suffer the awful short form Phil.

Pippa (f)
See Philippa.

Pleasance, Pleasant (f)
Pretty old names derived from medieval French and meaning exactly what they appear to mean. Very rare in Britain today, but Pleasance is still occasionally found in the USA.

Polly (f)
See Pauline, Mary.

Primrose (f)
Theoretically, one of the most delightful of the flower and plant names which became popular around the turn of the century, Primrose can be disastrous. It only works if your daughter turns out small and dainty. I once knew a six-foot-tall Primrose who would have given anything to be called Jean or Mary.

Priscilla (f)
Now rather rare, which is not surprising as it is derived from the Latin word meaning 'ancient', Priscilla was one of the numerous New Testament names which became popular with the Puritans in the seventeenth century.

Prudence (f)
A virtue name which, although adopted by the Puritans, did not originate as a first name with them. It was already in use in the thirteenth century. Still used, it is frequently abbreviated to Pru.

Prunella (f)
In French, Prunella means 'prune coloured'. Are you surprised that it is not more popular?

Q

Queenie (f)
This was originally a pet name adopted with no connection between it and the given name, or used as a nickname for Regina, which means 'queen' in Latin. It was occasionally used as an independent forename in the nineteenth and early twentieth centuries, but now, thankfully, it appears to be obsolete.

Quentin, Quintin (m)
A French form of a Roman clan name, introduced to England after the Norman Conquest. It spread to other parts of Britain, and had died out everywhere except Scotland by the end of the Middle Ages. Quentin was revived during the nineteenth century thanks to the fame of the novel *Quentin Durward*. Traditionally, the name has sometimes been given to the fifth child in a family.

R

Rachel (f)
A lovely biblical name. In Hebrew it means 'ewe' – the symbol of gentle innocence. Its early use in this country was confined to Jewish families, but Christians took it up after the Reformation. An English spelling variation at this time was Rachael. It declined after a spell of popularity during the seventeenth century, but now, with all the other good old biblical names, it is enjoying a fashionable revival. Rachel has no short forms or nicknames, is still reasonably unusual, and has a long tradition.

Ralph (m)
In earlier times Ralph was occasionally spelled as Rafe, and almost always pronounced that way. Now that Ralph is the normal form, the older pronunciation has a certain snobbish tone – it's reminiscent of those people who pronounce golf as goff. Anyway, if this is your choice, make up your mind about the pronunciation because there is something to be said for either version. The name means 'counsel wolf' in Old Norse; Radulf was the original form. Raoul, the French variant, is still found occasionally in Britain, not as a medieval survival, but because it took the imagination of British soldiers in France during World War One.

Randal, Randolph (m)
Today Randal is still found in gipsy families, but is rare elsewhere. No one seems to love Randolph these days – possibly because of the modern connotations of the awful short form, Randy. Both names derive from the Old English Randwulf – 'shield-wolf'. 'Lord Randal My Son' was a delightfully sinister ballad popular during the Middle Ages. At this period the name was widely used, but it declined later. Randolph was coined as an 'ancient' name during the eighteenth century. In fact it was simply an adaption of the Latin form Randulfus.

Raoul (m)
See Ralph.

Raphael (m)
A name with great presence, seldom used outside Jewish families. Raphael was one of the archangels. The name means 'God has healed' in Hebrew.

Ray, Raymond (m)
Introduced to England by the Normans, Raymond was originally an Old German name meaning 'mighty protector'. It is still widely used in Britain, usually shortened to the pet form Ray.

Rebecca (f)
A beautiful Hebrew name with the unfortunate meaning

149

'heifer', which is best ignored. In the Bible, Rebecca was the beautiful wife of Isaac. After the Reformation the name became popular in Britain, sometimes spelled Rebekah. There is a very pretty short form, Becky, most perfectly embodied in Becky Sharp, the heroine of Thackeray's novel *Vanity Fair*.

Regina (f)
The Latin word meaning 'queen'. It probably came into use as a girl's name during the Middle Ages, when Mary was considered too sacred for everyday use. It is a contraction of Mary, Queen of Heaven. Names like Dolores and Mercedes developed in the same way. It is rare today. Queenie is sometimes used as a nickname.

Reginald (m)
Derived from the older first name Reynold, now obsolete. It means 'force' or 'power' in Old English. Neither form was ever common in the early days, and they declined after the Middle Ages. A nineteenth century revival put Reginald back into circulation, and today it is commonplace, although not fashionable. Reg and Reggie are the short forms.

René (m), *Renée* (f)
Two of the few successful foreign borrowings, these combine well with English surnames. They are derived from the Latin meaning 'born again', and, properly speaking, are French names. The one problem they present is that of pronunciation. The masculine version is all right, because when it is mis-pronounced it generally emerges as Rennie. The feminine is less fortunate, invariably becoming Reenie or, worse, the short form Reen.

Reuben (m)
A quietly attractive masculine name of biblical origin. In Hebrew it means 'behold, a son' – possibly the ideal choice for a male chauvinist parent! Reuben is very attractive and still unusual. In view of the current vogue for biblical names it could be ripe for revival. Beware of the short form, Rube.

Rex (m)
For some unknown reason, Rex always sounds a bit caddish – but in the nicest possible way. It is a modern forename, a direct adoption of the Latin word meaning 'king'.

Rhoda (f)
Used as a Christian name in Britain since the seventeenth century, Rhoda is derived from the Greek word meaning 'rose'. It is fairly unusual today.

Rhodri (m)
A traditional Welsh name, now being gradually replaced in Wales by Roderick and very seldom encountered at all outside the Principality. It means 'crown ruler'.

Rhona (f)
See Rowena.

Rhys (m)
A common Welsh forename which gave rise to such surnames as Rees, Rice, Price and Preece. The latter two surnames developed from the Welsh custom of surnaming each generation 'son of' – hence ap Rhys, which became Preece. Rhys declined somewhat as a forename earlier this century, but the increasing popularity of Welsh and Celtic names has led to its revival. It means 'rashness'.

Richard (m)
One of the most popular English masculine names ever since its introduction by the Normans. As long as you can prevent use of the outdated and overused short form Dick, Richard is a sturdy and dignified name. If you like short forms, there is the much more attractive medieval pet version, Dickon. Ric was another early short form. Richie is as bad as Dick. The name, derived from Old German, means 'hard ruler'.

Rita (f)
Originally an abbreviation of Margarita, Rita has been used as a separate name in modern times.

151

Robert (m), *Roberta, Robina* (f)
One of the old faithful traditional names. Like Richard,
Robert has the drawback of a universal short form which has
impeded the use of the full name for centuries. In this case
it is Bob. Apart from the fact that lots of people call their
dogs Bob, it is far too commonplace to be used in place of
the full version. Rob and Robbie are preferable if people
must shorten it, but do try to stop them. Robert is too good
a name to waste. It has Old English origins and means 'fame-
bright'. The separate name Robin started out as a diminutive
of Robert. If you want a slight variation, you could try the
Middle English form Robard, but if you do, be prepared for
everyone to spell it incorrectly. Roberta and Robina, the
feminine forms, appeared fairly early, but have always been
more popular in Scotland than elsewhere.

Robin (m and f)
Originally a pet form of Robert, now often used as a separate
name. Its adoption as a feminine form is probably associated
with the bird of that name.

Roderick (m)
This is derived from the original Old German Hrodric –
'fame rule'. Roderick has always been more popular in Scotland than elsewhere. Like Rodney, it is invariably shortened
to Roddy.

Rodney (m)
A surname, adopted from the name of a Somerset village,
which in turn became a forename after Admiral Rodney,
who made it famous during the eighteenth century. The
place name means 'reed island'. Usually shortened to Roddy.

Roger (m)
Roger was very popular during the Middle Ages, so much so
that it became too commonplace and eventually fell into
disuse. At one point its traditional short form, Hodge, was
regarded as a synonym for peasant. It was revived during the
nineteenth century and today is widely used without being
too commonplace. Rodge has replaced Hodge as the usual

short form, but is far less attractive than the full name. It means 'fame spear' in Old English.

Roland, Rowland (m)
Roland was the greatest of Charlemagne's paladins. He was killed at a great battle, defending the Pyrenean pass of Roncesvalles against his master's enemies. His story was told in one of the most famous of the medieval romances, the *Chanson de Roland*, and through it the name became very popular during the Middle Ages. The original English spelling was Rowland; Roland is a modern attempt to 'historicise' the name, but is now the version most generally used. Roland is graceful, attractive, and relatively unusual; in fact a perfect forename as long as you manage to avoid the awful short form Rowly.

Rolf, Rollo (m)
Rolf is the original Norman and, later, English form, Rollo the Latinised version. Both have an indefinably aristocratic air, unless your son's name is mispronounced as Row-low and instantly gives people an image of a popular brand of chocolate. It is correctly pronounced when it rhymes with follow. The name derives from the Old German 'fame wolf'. Rolf is little used today, having disappeared fairly early because of its resemblance to the more popular Ralph. Rollo came into use in the nineteenth century and still appears occasionally.

Roma (f)
Like Florence, the name of the Italian city, has been adopted as a girl's forename, but it is not particularly enterprising and lacking in tradition and distinction.

Ronald (m)
A Scottish version of Reginald which has now spread outside Scotland. It has awful short forms: Ron and Ronnie.

Rory (m)
A modern Irish version of the Gaelic Ruaidhri, meaning 'red'. Roy is a shortened form, now often encountered as a separate name.

153

Rosa (f)
See Rose.

Rosalie (f)
An Italian and French name occasionally used in England,
but quite rare. It is derived from the name of the ancient
ceremony of hanging garlands of roses on tombs – Rosalia
in Latin.

Rosalind (f)
Originally Rosalind had the unpromising meaning 'horse
serpent' in Old German, but it was adopted in Spain, where
it was mistakenly interpreted as Spanish for 'pretty rose'. Its
use in Britain is due to Shakespeare's adoption of the name
for a character in *As You Like It*. It has a smart ring and is
unusual without being outrageous. Try to stop people from
calling her Roz.

Rosamund, Rosamond (f)
Another name, like Rosalind, with horsy German origins,
which was cleaned up by the attribution of different roots.
In this case the name was said to come from the Latin 'pure
rose'. The French form, Rosamond, briefly superseded the
English Rosamund during the eighteenth century. Both are
used today. Roz is the short form.

Rose (f)
Possibly the prettiest of the flower names (although some
unromantic souls insist on identifying it with the Old German
word for 'horse'!). Rose has been used in Britain since the
Middle Ages. The Latin form Rosa, less common in this
country, is even more attractive. It can be an unfortunate
choice unless the bearer grows up to be a pretty woman.
Rose is impossible to shorten, so, perversely, people are apt
to lengthen it to Rosie. Don't let them. The foreign diminutives Rosetta and Rosina also appear.

Rosanna (f)
A mixture of Rose and Anna, coined in the eighteenth century. Today it is more popular in Italy than in this country,
but it is pretty.

Rosemary (f)
Adopted from the plant of that name in the eighteenth century. It did not come into general use until the twentieth century. The plant name is derived from Latin and means 'sea-dew'. It is possible that as a girl's name, Rosemary has no connection with the plant, and is simply a combination of Rose and Mary.

Rowena (f)
A medieval name coined from the Old English words meaning 'famed friend'. It did not become popular until Sir Walter Scott used it for the heroine of his novel *Ivanhoe*.

Rowland (m)
See Roland.

Roy (m)
See Rory.

Ruby (f)
Like Pearl and Beryl, ruby was one of the precious stones which lent their names to girls at the turn of the last century. All are very old-fashioned today.

Rudolf (m)
A modern German version of an old name with the same roots as Rolf. It has occasionally been borrowed in Britain, but a 1950s' popular song about a red-nosed reindeer of that name has probably ruined its future.

Rupert (m)
A relentlessly upper class name introduced by Prince Rupert of the Rhine, nephew of Charles I. Modern admirers of the soldier prince tend to bestow it on their unfortunate offspring. It has the same roots as the more conventional Robert.

Russell (m)
This started out as a nickname based on the French for 'red', became an aristocratic surname and was adopted in modern times as a forename.

155

Ruth (f)
A beautiful biblical name of obscure meaning. Until the Reformation its use was confined to Jewish families. Now it is popular with non-Jews too. It is simple, lovely and dignified. It also combines well with just about any surname. Of course, people are unable to resist the temptation to meddle with it. Unable to devise a short form, they tend to resort to Ruthie as a pet name.

S

Sadie (f)
See Sarah.

Sally (f)
Originally a pet form of Sarah, now well established as a separate name. Both forms are attractive; but if you are going to call the child Sally all her life, don't have her christened Sarah. It is pointless.

Salome (f)
A gorgeous name, but who could get away with it? It is impossible to match to a surname: in Salome's day they didn't use them. Even if you did have the nerve to use it, your unfortunate daughter would probably shorten it to Sal in self-defence. Better leave it to the Bible and other literary sources. Incidentially, it means 'peace of Zion'.

Samantha (f)
I am still haunted by the memory of hearing, across a crowded British sea-front, a shrill maternal voice crying: 'Come 'ere, our Samantha!' In the 1950s, it was a beautiful name, seldom used. Then it joined the ranks of Melanie and Emma as one of the Names of the Decade. It has since died of overwork. Perhaps it will be coming up for revival when

your grandchildren are parents-to-be. At present it is best left on the shelf.

Sam(p)son (m)
As well as the biblical tradition, the use in Britain of Samson owes its origins to a similar Celtic name. In spite of this joint heritage, it appears to have died out completely in this country towards the end of the seventeenth century. Today the name has something of the circus strong-man about it, an obvious influence of the Old Testament story. Perhaps this explains its lack of popularity in an age when other biblical names are being revived enthusiastically. It means 'sun-child' in Hebrew.

Samuel (m)
A biblical name which is right out of fashion today. Samuel was the greatest of the Old Testament prophets. It was extremely popular from the Reformation until early this century, then it went out of style. Like the once over-popular girls' names, Ada, Gertrude and Bertha, it is probably unpopular primarily because it is automatically associated with the older generation. The name means 'name of God'. Sam and Sammy are the common abbreviations.

Sanchia (f)
Very pretty, slightly exotic-sounding name imported to Britain via Spain and Provence. Originally Sanchia derived from the Latin word meaning 'holy'. In the Middle Ages, when it was first introduced to England, it was sometimes confused with Cynthia. Sanchia seems almost an ideal modern choice. It is very unusual, has a long tradition and is hard to shorten. It can be a little unfortunate with certain surnames – generally speaking, plain ones work best with it – but apart from that it offers few pitfalls.

Sandra (f)
A diminutive of the Italian Alessandra, used in modern times as a separate name. The full English equivalent of the name – Alexandra – is much more attractive.

157

Sandy (f)
Pet form of Sandra.

Sara(h) (f)
One of the best of all girls' names, and currently enjoying great popularity. In Hebrew it means 'princess'. The original Sarah was Abraham's wife. The name has been used in Britain since the twelfth century and became really popular after the Reformation. In the seventeenth century an odd variation, Sarey, was often found; and later Sarah was used to form the compound name Saranna. Sally is a favourite pet form, but if you prefer this, use it as the proper name. There is no point in baptising a child Sarah, then calling her Sally. Another diminutive, Sadie, has a somewhat raffish image (c.f. Miss Sadie Thomson in Somerset Maugham's *Rain*). In Ireland Sarah has been used sometimes to anglicise Sorcha and Saraid.

Saul (m)
The name of the first king of Israel. With appropriate symbolism, it means 'asked for' in Hebrew. It was also St Paul's name before his conversion to Christianity. Saul has been used very occasionally as a forename, but has never been popular.

Sean (m)
Irish form of John now found in other parts of Britain too.

Sebastian (m)
The name that has everything if you are looking for distinction, panache and an aristocratic air. Sebastian has always hovered on the borders of trendies without suffering the over-exposure which degraded Dominic and Benedict. The name is derived from the Greek word meaning 'venerable'. Sebastian became popular during the Middle Ages because the saint of that name was a favourite subject of medieval art. He had been martyred by being shot with arrows.

Secundus (m)
Latin for 'second', Secundus came into use as a name when the parents had large families in Victorian days and rejoiced

in naming them anything up to Septimus, Octavius and Decimus depending on how many sons preceded them. Secundus occurs far enough down the scale to fit in with the smaller modern family unit, but it is hard to imagine the name making a come-back.

Selina (f)
A pretty name of obscure origin which appears to have evolved during the seventeenth century. It is probably an English version of the French Celine, which is derived from the Latin word for 'heaven'. Selina has never been common, but it still occurs occasionally. It is likely to be shortened to Lina.

Selwyn (m)
Rare even in the early days, Selwyn is an Old English name which died out and was revived in the nineteenth century, when it became particularly popular in Wales. It means 'house friend'. It is not popular today. In Wales it has produced the deadly short form Sel.

Septimus (m)
Latin for 'seventh'; bestowed on the seventh son in Victorian days. Secundus, Octavius and Decimus were also used.

Seraphina (f)
A delightful derivation from the Hebrew 'burning one'. It became popular in Europe as a saint's name and has always been rare.

Serena (f)
Means exactly what it appears to mean – 'serene one'. Although it has been known since medieval times, it has always been rare.

Seth (m)
Stella Gibbons's hilarious book *Cold Comfort Farm* delivered the *coup de grace* on Seth. She used it as the name of the strong, silent Adonis in a send-up of the rural novels which were popular in the 1920s. The name means 'compen-

sation', and the original bearer was supposedly the son born to Adam and Eve after Abel's death.

Shane (m)
An anglicised rendering of the Irish version of John, Sean. Avoid it. If you like the name, use the correct Irish spelling. Shane conjures up pictures of the hero of the all time great cowboy movie. It sounded good on Alan Ladd, but he wasn't Shane Anybody – just Shane.

Sheila(gh) (f)
A phonetic version of the Irish Sile. Sheila has become popular in England, too. In the nineteenth century it was frequently changed to Julia in Ireland. Sile was derived from Cecilia, the patron saint of music.

Sheena (f)
An anglicised form of Sine, the Gaelic version of Jane.

Shirley (f)
This started out as a surname, derived in turn from a place name meaning 'shire meadow'. In the mid-nineteenth century Charlotte Bronte used it as the forename of a heroine and set a fashion. Shirley received a boost in the 1930s due to the popularity of the child film star Shirley Temple. As a result of over-use at that time, it is not popular today.

Sibyl (f)
A modern spelling of a name which has appeared down the centuries variously as Sibylla, Sibella and Sibley. The Sibyls were allegedly women who acted as mouthpieces of God. A fairly unusual name today. Discourage the dreadful short form, Sib.

Sidney (m)
Originally an aristocratic surname derived from the French St Denis, which eventually became a forename. The alternative spelling Sydney did not appear before the nineteenth century. The short form Sid was possibly responsible for the name's eclipse in modern times.

160

Sigrid (f)
This name, with Old Norse origins, is still popular in Scandinavia. There were English versions in the Middle Ages, but they died out quite early and when it appears today it is borrowed from modern Scandinavian. It is derived from a word meaning 'victory'.

Silvia, Sylvia (f)
Shakespeare used Sylvia in his *Two Gentlemen of Verona*, which probably popularised it in England. Previously Silvia had been an Italian forename. It is the feminine form of the Latin Silvius 'of the wood'.

Simeon (m)
See Simon.

Simon (m)
A very popular New Testament name which was equally favoured in Medieval England because it was St Peter's forename. Many English surnames derive from it. Like Peter, Simon declined after the Reformation. It has become fashionable during the later part of this century. The name means 'harkening' in Hebrew. Simeon, kept separate in medieval versions of the Bible, was probably the same name in the Hebrew version.

Solomon (m)
The name of one of Israel's greatest kings, a byword for wisdom. Solomon – generally spelled Salamon – was popular in Britain during the Middle Ages and again in the seventeenth century. Today it seems to be used exclusively by Jewish families. Solly is the usual short form. The name means 'little man of peace'.

Sonia (f)
A pretty Russian diminutive of Sophia, used in Britain since the 1920s when it featured in a popular novel.

Sophia, Sophie (f)
Currently one of the smartest girls' names around, in either version, but with Sophie probably having a slight edge.

Sophia is the original Greek version – it means 'wisdom' – and Sophie the anglicised form. It was used in England as early as the seventeenth century, but came into its own in Georgian days because it was a favourite with the German royal house. It went out of fashion in the late nineteenth century and remained unpopular until a few years ago. Now its popularity is increasing constantly.

Stanley (m)
Originally a surname derived from a common place name, Stanley became popular as a forename in the nineteenth century in deference to the explorer Henry Morton Stanley. As with so many Victorian favourites, it rapidly became over-exposed and is nowadays very unfashionable. Stan is the universal short form.

Stella (f)
A direct adoption of the Latin word meaning 'star', Stella was used as a forename as early as the Middle Ages, but undoubtedly derives its modern popularity from frequent use in literature. It is pretty, unaffected and relatively uncommon.

Stephanie (f), *Stephen, Steven* (m)
Stephen was the first Christian martyr. The name was quite common in Greece, but did not become popular in England until after the Norman Conquest. It means 'crown'. Stephanie is the French feminine form, which has been used in this country in modern times. It is an attractive name. Unfortunately the short forms Steve and Stevie are apt to be used indiscriminately for boys and girls. In America the pet form Steffie occurs.

Stuart (m)
A name derived from the Old English version of the word 'steward'. The royal house of Scotland was founded by a High Steward named Walter. Stewart was originally the surname of that royal house, the spelling changing to Stuart in the sixteenth and early seventeenth centuries. Both spellings were adopted as forenames as a sign of affection for the House, and of loyalty to the Scottish cause during the eigh-

teenth century. Today it appears as a popular forename throughout Britain, usually spelled Stuart.

Susan(nah) (f)
The older form, Susannah, is prettier than Susan, and Shushannah, the Hebrew original, is better than either. It means 'lily'. Susannah was the heroine of the *Apocrypha Book of Susannah and the Elders*. The name became popular in England during the seventeenth century, as Shusanna and Susanney. By the eighteenth century Susan was more usual, and has remained so. Sue is a bland, boring short form; Sukey has more character, but neither can beat the full version, Susannah. Nowadays the French form, Suzanne, occurs in Britain too.

Sybil (f)
The wrong way to spell Sibyl.

Sylvia (f)
See Silvia.

T

Tabitha (f)
An attractive name found in the New Testament. It has fallen from favour over the years, but could make a comeback on the wave of popularity for Biblical names. In Aramaic Tabitha means 'gazelle'. In the New Testament story, Tabitha was very charitable, and the name has usually been associated with help for the poor. The charitable image has been associated even more closely with Dorcas, the Greek rendering of Tabitha.

Talbot (m)
Still occasionally found as a forename, Talbot is more usually a surname. It probably derived from a derisive nickname of French origin, meaning 'woodcutter'.

Talitha (f)
Like Colleen, Talitha started out simply as the word for 'girl' – this time in Aramaic. It has been used this century as a forename, but only rarely.

Tamasine, Tamsin (f)
See Thomasin.

Tatiana (f)
A very popular Russian girl's name. The original Tatiana was a Christian martyr, venerated in the Orthodox Church. In Britain the unattractive short form Tanya is more popular than the full version.

Terence (m)
Initially Terence was found as a forename only in Ireland, where it was used to transliterate the unwieldly Toirdhealbhach. Now it has spread to England and is quite commonplace. Terry and Tel are the short forms. The origin of the name is obscure. We appear to have derived it from the name of the Roman clan Terentius.

Teresa, Theresa, Tessa (f)
An old name of unknown origin and meaning. Teresa was an early favourite in Spain, but did not spread until the renown of St Teresa of Avila took it to other Catholic countries in the sixteenth and seventeenth centuries. Admirers of the Austrian empress Maria Theresa introduced it to England in the eighteenth century. The short forms Tess and Tessa are popular, the latter existing as a name in its own right. None of the variations is fashionable, although all except Theresia are fairly commonplace. Teresa shares the modern diminutive, Terry, with the masculine name Terence.

Thelma (f)
Thelma was invented in the nineteenth century as the name of the heroine in a Marie Corelli novel. It has been used regularly since then, and is more popular in the USA than in Britain.

Theobald (m)
The ultimate in unfashionable names, possibly because the final syllable automatically conjures up images of baldness. In fact, 'bald' is Old German for 'bold'. The vernacular version, Tybalt, is rather more attractive, but no variation is common today.

Theodora (f), *Theodore* (m)
A translation of the Greek 'God's gift'. The name has been used, rarely, in Britain since the seventeenth century. It is believed that the Welsh Tudor or Tewdwr developed from Theodore. Both sexes usually abbreviate it to Theo. In the USA, where it is rather more popular, Teddy is the standard short form.

Theophania (f)
This, the Latin version of the name, is not particularly attractive; but translated to vernacular English in the thirteenth century as Tiffany, it formed one of the prettiest of all girls' names. In Latin it means 'the manifestation of God', and was generally given to girls born during Epiphany. In Cornwall it was even transliterated into Epiphany from time to time.

Thirza (f)
An Old Hebrew name derived from a city. It developed strong lower-class associations during the nineteenth century thanks to the popularity of *The Death of Abel*, a work in which a woman called Thirza appeared, setting a fashion among working people. It is very unusual today.

Thomas (m)
An old name enjoying an enormous revival of popularity. Thomas is once again a firm fixture in *The Times*'s top ten boys' names. Thomas has been among the commonest men's names in England since the Middle Ages – hence the saying 'every Tom, Dick and Harry'. It suffered a decline in the early twentieth century and its present fashionable revival began in the mid-1970s. It originated as an Aramaic nickname for 'twin'. The real name of Thomas the Apostle was Judah. As he was a twin, he was nicknamed Thomas to

distinguish him from the other two Judahs, St Jude, brother of James, and Judah of Kerioth – Judas Iscariot. The old short form, Tom, is also fashionable at present in its own right, along with other clipped, butch diminutives like Jake and Ben. In France the usual abbreviations were Mace or Macey. Tommy gained currency as a nickname for British soldiers because the enlistment form for private soldiers in the nineteenth century bore the specimen signature Tommy Atkins. In Scotland Tam and Tammy are popular short forms.

Thomasin(e) (f)
The feminine diminutive of Thomas, found in Britain since the fourteenth century. Thomasina was an early variation. In Cornwall it evolved as Tamasine or Tamsin, and the latter form has become quite fashionable in modern Britain. The Americans have adopted Tammy, here a masculine diminutive used in Scotland, as a feminine name, and it has been used very occasionally in this country.

Thora (f)
A very rare survivor of the masculine Thor, which has disappeared altogether in England. Even Thora is seldom used. Thor, the Norse god of thunder, gave his name to Thursday, so if you want to use the name and have a daughter born on Thursday, it's appropriate.

Timothy (m)
Fashion in names in sixteenth century Britain was not unlike that of today. Both classical and biblical names suddenly became popular and it was at this period that Timothy first came into vogue. It means 'honour God', and was the name of St Paul's companion, to whom two of the Epistles were addressed. It is extremely popular and quite fashionable. Tim, with Timmy the common short form, is acceptable nowadays as a name in its own right.

Tobias, Toby (m)
Tobias is seldom used today. Toby, on the other hand, is decidedly trendy. The names are, respectively, the Greek and English forms of an Old Hebrew original meaning 'the

Lord is good'. Mr Punch's dog, Toby, is so called in memory
of the dog in the Apocrypha story of Tobias and the Angel.
Toby Philpott, a great eighteenth century drinker, is remembered with the traditional Toby jug.

Toinette (f)
See Anthony.

Tristram, Tristan (m)
One of the great romantic names, thanks to the Tristan and
Isolde legend. It is derived from the Celtic Drystan, 'tumult',
but the French form, Tristan, was also influenced by the
French word for 'sad'. The usual form in England was
Tristram. Both variations are still used, but are rare. Use
with caution. It demands a swashbuckling surname.

Trixie (f)
See Beatrix.

U

Ulla (f)
Very occasionally found in Britain, this name derives from
the Old English meaning 'owl'.

Ulric (m), *Ulrica* (f)
A modern rendering of the Old English Wulfric – 'wolf
ruler'. When surnames came into use it evolved into names
like Woolrich and Woolridge. The current form, used only
rarely, is probably derived from the Norman French version.
Ulrica is a straight borrowing from modern German, and is
slightly more common.

Ulysses (m)
Almost unknown in England, Ulysses is still used in Ireland,
generally as a translation of the Irish Ulick. Ulysses is the

Roman translation of the name of Odysseus, the Greek hero
of the Trojan War whose wanderings are described in
Homer's epic poem, *The Odyssey*.

Una (f)
An anglicised version of the Irish Oonagh, 'lamb'. It is also
found in English as Winifred and, translated, as Agnes.
The poet Spenser also uses Una as a derivation of the Latin
word for 'one'.

Unity (f)
Another Puritan virtue name, once popular but seldom
found today. Best-known modern holder of the name was
probably Unity Mitford, who formed a sort of one-woman
fan club for Adolph Hitler.

Urith (f)
A variation of Hierytha, patron saint of the church of
Chettlehampton in Devon. It was used from the early seven-
teenth century as a local forename, and still survives in the
Trevelyan family.

Ursula (f)
A fairly common name in the Middle Ages, due to the
popular legend of St Ursula, a Cornish princess who was
shipwrecked and killed near Cologne in the fifth century.
After a decline, it became popular again in the nineteenth
century, but is not favoured today. It is derived from the
Latin meaning 'little she-bear'.

V

Valentine (m and f)
A natural for children of either sex born on February 14.
For once, even the diminutive, Val, is attractive. Valentine is

derived from the Latin word meaning 'strong and healthy'. The feast day of Valentine the Roman martyr almost coincided with that of Juno Februata, when lots were drawn for lovers. The custom was transferred from the pagan to the Christian religious festival as part of the Church's policy of absorbing older rites. Valentine has never been a common name, but has been used occasionally in Britain since the twelfth century. It was exclusively a man's name until the seventeenth century, but since then has been used indiscriminately for either sex.

Valeria, Valerie (f), *Valerian* (m)
Of the three, only Valerie is currently much used. The Roman clan name Valerius was the original development. Valeria is the Italian feminine form. Valerie was not used in Britain before the nineteenth century, when it was imported from France. Valerian is rarely found in Britain. It is used by the Wellesleys as a traditional family forename. Valerie is frequently abbreviated to Val.

Vanessa (f)
Like Wendy, a literary invention. This one was devised by Dean Swift, as a partial anagram of Esther Vanhomrigh. It has been used occasionally since then, but is quite unusual.

Venetia (f)
A very elegant name, said to be the Latinised version of the Welsh Gwyneth.

Vera (f)
This is relatively modern as a British forename. It came into use in the second half of the nineteenth century. Vera is derived from the Russian Vjera, meaning 'Faith'. Its popularity in Victorian Britain resulted from use of the name by Ouida in her novel *Moths*. It is still in use, but currently out of fashion.

Vere (m)
Originally adopted as a family forename from the surname de Vere, this was later used by people with no connection to

the original bearers. The surname derived from Ver in Normandy. Vere has very occasionally been used as a feminine name.

Verena (f)
Verena was a virgin martyr in the reign of Diocletian. Her cult became very popular in Switzerland, and many churches around Lucerne are dedicated to her. As this region became a popular centre for English tourists, the name was brought back to Britain. It has never been widely used.

Verity (f)
One of the 'virtue' names which became popular with the Puritans in seventeenth century England. Although not fashionable, it has an attractive and dignified image and cannot be readily adapted to nicknames.

Vernon (m)
Another forename which originated as a surname. It was first used as a forename in the nineteenth century. Vernon is a very common French place-name and this is undoubtedly where the British version originated.

Veronica (f)
Originally the name of the cloth which allegedly retained the image of Christ after it had been used to wipe His face. Later it was mistakenly thought to be the name of the woman who had wiped His face. It has been fairly widely used as a girl's name in Britain since the nineteenth century.

Vesta (f)
Vesta was the Roman goddess of fire to whom the Vestal Virgins dedicated their lives. It has occasionally appeared as a forename in modern times.

Victor (m)
A direct derivation from the Latin for 'conquerer', it was used in medieval England, but only rarely, and appears to have become popular during the nineteenth century, presumably as a masculine version of Victoria.

Victoria (f)
This did not become as popular as may be imagined in nine-teenth century Britain. Queen Victoria was named after her German mother, and Victoria passed on to her numerous godchildren, but it declined quickly and has become popular only quite recently. It has appeared in *The Times*'s top ten girls' names for some years. Vicky was a popular early diminutive, but Tory is a less commonplace short form. Vicky and Vicki have become separate names in modern times. Victoria is Latin for 'victory'.

Vincent (m)
An elegant old forename too often spoiled by the ghastly diminutive Vince. Vincent is derived from the Latin meaning 'conquering'. The name has occurred in England since the thirteenth century, but has been most popular since the nineteenth century.

Viola (f)
The beguiling heroine of Shakespeare's *Twelfth Night* was undoubtedly responsible for the surge of popularity enjoyed by this name. It is the Latin word for 'violet'. Pretty and unusual, but expect people to call the bearer Vi and try to dissuade them.

Violet (f)
Derives from the Old French diminutive of Viola, Violete. French influence in Scotland resulted in adoption of the French form Violette there, but in England Violet was the usual spelling. It became popular during the nineteenth cen-tury but is now unfashionable. Again, there will be trouble with Vi.

Virginia (f)
Not derived, as might be expected, from 'virginal', but from a Roman clan name, Verginius. It has become more popular in the USA than in Britain, probably thanks to the State name, originally given to a plantation in honour of Queen Elizabeth I. Ginny and Virgie, the usual short forms, are unprepossessing.

Vivian (m), *Vivien* (f)
The masculine form is derived from the Latin Vivianus –
'alive', but it is believed that Tennyson devised the feminine
version from the French form Vivienne. Both are pleasant,
and fairly unusual. Viv is the common abbreviation.

W

Waldo (m)
Be warned: it's derived from the Old German words for
'strong thief'. Waldo is a derivation of Waltheof, which is
now obsolete. Even Waldo is very seldom found today.

Wallace (m)
Started life as a Scottish surname and was adopted as a forename as a mark of respect for William Wallace, the famous
patriot. Its use has now spread outside Scotland.

Walter (m)
Introduced to Britain by the Normans, Walter has been in
use ever since. It originated in the Old German words 'rule'
and 'folk'. Wat was the original diminutive, but Walt is now
more usual.

Wanda (f)
An Ouida novel, published late last century, led to a popular
revival of this old name, which is still quite popular. It is
derived from the Old German for 'stock' or 'stem'.

Warner (m)
In Britain, Warner is now found primarily as a surname, but
it started out as a forename and is still quite popular as
such in the USA. It is an Old German name, meaning
'Varin's folk'. The surname Garner also derives from it.

Warren (m)
An Old German name of obscure meaning, derived from the name Varin. It is very rare in Britain today, although quite widely used in the USA.

Wendy (f)
A modern forename devised by J. M. Barrie as a pet-name for a friend's daughter – 'Friendy-Wendy' and later adopted in his play *Peter Pan* in 1904. It is still quite popular.

Wilfred, Wilfrid (m)
An old name revived during the nineteenth century and still quite commonplace, though unfashionable. Its origins are Old English, combining the words for 'will' and 'peace'. The two diminutives, Wilf and Fred, do not sparkle.

Wilhelmina (f)
A clumsy feminine form of Wilhelm, a nineteenth century borrowing from Germany. See William for derivation. The diminutive, Mina, is rather more attractive. Neither form is much used today.

William (m)
A sturdy old name which has bounced back to enormous popularity after years in the doldrums. From the sixteenth to the nineteenth centuries, William was the most common man's name in England, usually tying with John. Its origins are Old German, from the words for 'will' and 'helmet'.

Wilmot (f)
A charming feminine form of William, which died out as a forename early in the eighteenth century, but still survives as a surname. It is attractive enough to deserve revival.

Winifred (f)
An anglicised version of the Welsh Gwenfrewi, the name of a martyred princess. It is still used, but is becoming rarer. The short forms, Winnie and Freda are unattractive.

Winston (m)
Surprisingly, this name, now famous, was once used only by

the Churchill family. It was the maiden name of the grand-mother of the first Duke of Marlborough. The original Winston was a hamlet near Cirencester.

Y

Yolande (f)
This was developed in the Middle Ages from Violante, which in turn had derived from Viola. Jolenta and Joleicia were early variations, now obsolete. Yolande is still used occasionally.

Yorick (m)
Shakespeare coined this in *Hamlet*, probably as an anglicised version of the Danish Georg (pronounced Yorg). Although very rare, it is still used in Britain.

Yvonne, Yvette (f)
Derived from the feminine form of the French Yvon, in turn derived from the Old German for 'yew tree'. In modern times, Yvonne has been widely used in Britain. Yvette is less common. A pretty early version in England was Ivetta.

Z

Zacchaeus (m)
From the Aramaic word for 'pure', this forename was very popular in seventeenth century England but has fallen into disuse since. It is still found occasionally in the USA.

Zacharias, Zachary (m)
Another biblical name which became popular with the Puritans in the seventeenth century. Zachary has survived, but is very rare. It could be ripe for revival as the more popular biblical names become over-exposed. It is derived from the Hebrew 'Jehovah has remembered', and was the name of a king of Israel. Ringo Starr used the short form, Zak, for his son.

Zenobia (f)
A splendidly sexy name, originally belonging to a famous queen of Palmyra. Its meaning is obscure. Sadly, it is virtually unusable with modern surnames. For some reason it became popular in Cornwall late in the sixteenth century, when it evolved as Zenobe.

Zillah (f)
A favourite gipsy name, its origins are Hebrew. Zillah means 'shade'. It has been used occasionally outside Romany society.

Zoë (f)
A Greek version of Eve, it means 'life'. Although it is an ancient name, it was not adopted in Britain until the nineteenth century, and has been used occasionally ever since.